Transition to 21st Century Healthcare

A Guide for Leaders and Quality Professionals

Transition to 21st Century Healthcare

A Guide for Leaders and Quality Professionals

Scott Goodwin

CRC Press
Taylor & Francis Group
Boca Raton London New York

CRC Press is an imprint of the
Taylor & Francis Group, an **informa** business

A PRODUCTIVITY PRESS BOOK

CRC Press
Taylor & Francis Group
6000 Broken Sound Parkway NW, Suite 300
Boca Raton, FL 33487-2742

Printed on acid-free paper
Version Date: 20150126

International Standard Book Number-13: 978-1-4987-2687-0 (Hardback)

Library of Congress Cataloging-in-Publication Data

Goodwin, Scott, author.
  Transition to 21st century healthcare : a guide for leaders and quality professionals / Scott Goodwin.
    p. ; cm.
  Transition to twenty-first century healthcare
  Includes bibliographical references and index.
  ISBN 978-1-4987-2687-0 (alk. paper)
  I. Title. II. Title: Transition to twenty-first century healthcare.
  [DNLM: 1. Delivery of Health Care--trends--United States. 2. Delivery of Health Care--history--United States. 3. Health Care Reform--trends--United States. 4. History, 20th Century--United States. 5. History, 21st Century--United States. 6. Quality of Health Care--trends--United States. W 84 AA1]

RA418.3.U6
362.10973--dc23   2015001821

Visit the Taylor & Francis Web site at
http://www.taylorandfrancis.com

and the CRC Press Web site at
http://www.crcpress.com

To God for His grace to me in my
Lord and Savior, Jesus Christ,

and

To my wife, BJ, for her love and support through the years

Contents

Introduction

Transition to 21st century healthcare! This is not an option; it is survival for healthcare organizations and for high-quality healthcare in the communities they serve. Understanding what this means is the difference between organizations and leaders who survive and thrive and those that fail and disappear. If that sounds like a threat to you, then you are the one this guide can help.

The transition occurring in healthcare is seismic. American healthcare initially emerged from the fires of the first and second industrial revolutions. Many hospitals across the country still look like factories decaying in the Rust Belt of America: massive buildings designed for mass production. Industry moved on decades ago, but American healthcare did not. American healthcare was held back by its inability to transition to a new model.

Secure in its post-World War II dominance, American industry faced the onslaught of foreign competition in the late 20th century unprepared. The results are well known: massive disruption and economic devastation. The fires of competition burned away the assumptions of the past and ignited the transformation of American industry. The scars still remain and the transformation continues.

American healthcare travels the same path, but progress so far has been slow. Wrapped in the mythology of its past and secure behind the walls of its palatial hospital factories, healthcare in America asserts its superiority in the face of rising doubt. Protected by history and oceans and defended by its massive industrial structure of insurance, Big Pharma, big tech, big systems and organizational and professional sovereignty, change appears from the outside to lap against the walls of American healthcare like waves in a moat. What can possibly threaten the titanic structure of American healthcare?

It is not a foreign threat that confronts American healthcare, but rather a close and familiar companion: American industry. There is a sense of comfort among healthcare leaders as they confer with their supporters from industry who have paid the cost of care for years. Everyone knows the changes in the industrial sector and the strides America made in regaining past glory. Inspired by the success of other industries, healthcare sees itself achieving similar results without the devastation and without giving up the cloak of clinical uniqueness that shields it from the ravages of markets and competition.

Even as healthcare comforts itself with these thoughts, the reality that belies this image is gnawing at the edges. The source of the disease is the oxymoronic phrase "healthcare customer." Embedded in an economy that is 70% consumer driven, industry experienced the destructive creativity of customers choosing differently. Unable to grasp the significance of this phenomenon on the horizon, healthcare leaders and quality professionals tweak their systems by adjusting to the requirements for regulatory reporting and posting scores on websites. At the same time, the people they declare are receiving the best healthcare in the world are chiseling away at the foundations by making different choices.

If what I have said has raised your sense of concern or at least piqued your interest, for the sake of the healthcare we all depend on, I urge you to continue reading. Help is on the way! This guide offers a view of the past that helps you to understand the roots of the changes that are coming. It provides an explanation of the dramatic shift that occurred at the end of the 20th century in the way healthcare in America functions. It gives you insights into the changes you are experiencing now and a view of the transitions to the future that lie ahead of you.

The most important thing to remember is that the events of today have a source that you can understand and a direction that you can follow. You can reset your orientation to the future and take an active role in shaping the direction of healthcare. You can guide your organization or your quality program into the new healthcare of the 21st century. *Transition to 21st Century Healthcare* is an imperative for all of us who work in healthcare to respond to if we are to lead successful 21st century healthcare organizations and to provide care in a new way.

To understand this new path and the transformation that is occurring in American healthcare, it is important to recognize that there have been key phases in the evolution of American healthcare since the beginning of the 20th century. American medicine and healthcare were shaped in the 20th century by American culture, industry, society and history into a unique structure and nature. In the early 21st century, the strengths of industry and the organizational weaknesses of healthcare converged into a new transitional phase in which the industrialized quality machine entered healthcare and initiated a transformation. It is this phase that we are currently experiencing and this convergence is the source of much of the confusion. As healthcare progresses through this transitional industrialization phase, ten critical transitions appear as bridges to the creation of 21st century healthcare. Fully embracing industrialization in healthcare is the right path to the future, because industrialization breaks down the barriers and points to the transitions. In the transitions, the images of 21st century healthcare appear and serve to direct and motivate the efforts to create the future.

This book provides the basic framework to help you understand the healthcare world we are experiencing today and the transitions that lead to the future. It describes the key foundations and structures of 20th century healthcare. It opens to

you the nature of the forces of industrialization that are currently at work revealing the transitions to the future. It presents the ten transitions and the guiding images that lead to
a new model of healthcare. Finally, it suggests a view of the
future that represents the completion of the transitions and
the beginning of a new phase in American healthcare. This is
your guide to creating 21st century healthcare and a map to
help you see the journey we are traveling into the future.

About the Author

Scott Goodwin has 20 years' experience as a healthcare quality professional that includes positions as hospital-based quality vice president and chief quality officer, quality consultant for multiple hospitals and currently as vice president/chief quality officer. In 2013, he completed his doctorate in leadership studies at Franklin Pierce University. Since 2013 he has been an adjunct professor at New England College in Henniker, New Hampshire, where he designs and teaches a course in Quality and Lean, in addition to courses in organizational ethics, health informatics and supply chain. He also designed and taught a course at Bay State College, Boston, Massachusetts.

In 2014 he received the innovator's award from the New Hampshire Foundation for Healthy Communities, which celebrates extraordinary ingenuity, creativity and skill in improving health and healthcare access, delivery or quality.

Mr. Goodwin's work as chair of the New Hampshire Health Care Quality Assurance Commission brought him into legislative session to assist elected officials and policy makers in discussions about the complex world of measuring health care quality. And he has worked to support the efforts of quality professionals across New Hampshire to improve delivery of care to patients in hospitals and ambulatory surgical centers.

Joining with quality professionals across the state, Goodwin has supported innovative and cost-saving approaches to improving care that include reducing infections, improving surgical safety and promoting organizational cultures that support high quality.

Mr. Goodwin was selected to present at the National Association for Healthcare Quality 2014 conference in Nashville, Tennessee, on the topic, "What's in a Name: The Importance of Metaphors in Quality Improvement."

Chapter 1

A Brief History of American Healthcare

1.1 Introduction

The first step in understanding what is happening in American healthcare today is to understand the factors that shaped American healthcare in the past. American healthcare in the 20th century developed in a unique way. The development of medical technology and the professionalization of the physician, the central role of the handwritten medical record in the processes of care and the payment processes of commercial and governmental insurers shaped American healthcare in the 20th century.

As medical technology appeared in ever more sophisticated forms and as universities and hospitals became the educational foundations of physicians, these two forces converged to form the powerful healthcare production system of the 20th century. Amazingly, this production system found its home in what had been the refuge of the destitute outcasts of society. In the hospital, the new technology of laboratory, radiology and aseptic surgery merged with the professional physician and nurse to create the hospital as the iconic symbol of scientific medicine and the central point in the delivery of healthcare for more than a century. Patients left their homes and came to this new factory of health and healing to take advantage of the wonders of scientific medicine.

Within the halls of the hospital, the physician reigned supreme as the architect of medicine and the professional guide to the secrets of healthcare. Using the handwritten medical record, the physician ordered the care of the patient and created the record of the battle against illness and injury. Anyone who needed to know what was happening with the patient or what was needed turned to this personal record of the physician as to a road map. Scrawled in the often illegible handwriting of a personal journal, the medical record held the central role in shaping the processes of healthcare for more than a century and formed the foundational contract of the professionalization of the physician.

Finally, the insurance payment processes adopted by employers and the government by the middle of the 20th century redesigned healthcare from a relationship between the physician and the patient and the hospital to a relationship in which the patient accepted whatever care was provided under the auspices of the insurance company paying the physician and the hospital. With no participation in the monetary exchange for healthcare services, the patient was lost in the pursuit of revenue. In place of the patient, a mythical apparatus grew up in which the hospitals created pricing and charges and negotiated with insurance companies while physicians wrote orders for testing and procedures that grew out of the new technology that was marketed to physicians and hospitals as tools for negotiations with insurance companies.

Beginning in simple forms in the mid-19th century, American healthcare grew up to reflect the culture, values, economics and industry of America in the 20th century. It is a fitting symbol of the strengths and weaknesses of a society that has tremendous capacity for innovation and industry and an amazing ability to fail in the routine tasks of providing healthcare services to its people. This perplexing dichotomy is exhibited in the saga of American healthcare as it evolved in the 20th century. This history is an important starting point for understanding American healthcare and the way it fits within American life.

The foundational developments of 20th century healthcare unfold in three formative areas. Section 1.2, "The Stethoscope and the AMA," identifies the essentials of the healthcare delivery system that solidified in the early years of the 20th century. Medical technology, symbolized by the stethoscope, evolved in the 18th and 19th centuries and came to full fruition in the early 20th century as it foreshadowed the redefining of the patient as an object of care rather than the partner of the physician. The technology of aseptic surgery, the laboratory and x-rays migrated to the hospital as a setting able to support them. Their presence re-created the hospital as the healthcare factory and patients left their homes and the familial structure of healing to come to the factory environment of the hospital to receive the benefits of this new technology. At the same time, the physicians using the new technology developed a new self-consciousness about their work and status. Beginning in the mid-19th century, the American Medical Association (AMA) defined this consciousness as a unique profession and organized medicine as a cultural, political and economic force was born. The iconic image of the physician with the stethoscope around the neck captures this convergence in a familiar symbol of the synergy that created American healthcare.

Section 1.3, "The Medical Record," traces the scrawl of the handwritten, hardcopy record across American healthcare processes in the hospital of 20th century America. The persistence of the handwritten medical record as a tool of the physician in the care of patients exerted a profound influence on the development of hospitals. The creation of, storage of and access to information about patients in the medical record shaped the work flows of healthcare throughout the modern period until the arrival of healthcare information technology and the Internet at the end of the 20th century. With the implementation of electronic information systems, the availability of information and the new organizational connections removed the handwritten record as a barrier to the emergence of a new model of healthcare.

Section 1.4, "The Money," describes the single most important motivation for change in healthcare. It is this element that defines American healthcare in a way completely different from that of the rest of the world. From common beginnings in the charity hospitals, the world accepted healthcare as a common right of people and a common responsibility of nations. America diverged from the rest of the world by limiting access to those who had the ability to pay for it. With the Great Depression, the need for patients encouraged hospitals to create prepayment plans to fill empty beds. During World War II, the need for workers prompted industry to offer hospital insurance as a benefit of employment. Finally, in the era of the Great Society, Medicare opened the doors of hospitals through government-funded hospital insurance to the elderly and the poor. The largess of industry and government in the form of cost-based insurance payments produced an unprecedented expansion of hospitals and healthcare technology. This golden era of healthcare growth threatened the competitiveness of American industry and the solvency of the US government and called forth the dragon of industrialization.

1.2 The Stethoscope and the AMA

The transformation of American medicine by technology can be seen in the appearance of the wooden tube known as the "stethoscope" in the early years of the 19th century. A hollow wooden instrument that could be mistaken for a magic wand or a musical pipe, the stethoscope literally came between the patient and the physician and transformed their relationship.

The move from immediate auscultation to mediate auscultation with the stethoscope not only made the examination
more palatable for the physician, who previously had to literally place his ear on the patient, but also subtly changed the
relationship between the patient and the physician. There was
now an intermediary in the form of a wooden tube. What
was so transformative about the stethoscope? How could
such a small and simple device serve as the harbinger of the
reshaping of healthcare by technology in the 20th century
(Roguin 2006)?

Prior to the stethoscope, the patients knew more than the
physician about their state of health. The physician required
the patient to be an active participant in the analysis of the
patient's health by responding to a series of questions from
the physician. The physician asked the questions, evaluated
the answers and examined the external state of the body, but
was locked out of the essential workings of the body. In this
situation, the ability to listen to the patient and to solicit information was of paramount importance. The patient as a person
was essential to the work of the physician. The story of the
illness was critically important information that could only
be obtained through the voluntary responses of the patient.
Examining the patient was problematic at best with hands
and eyes and pressing ears against the chest. The results
were limited.

The stethoscope, as will become a common theme
throughout this book, caused healthcare to change direction
through the subtle change of a wooden tube placed between
the patient and the physician. Like a small stone dislodged
and rolling down a hill causes other stones to be moved and
eventually a new landscape to be formed, the wooden tube
initiated changes that were transformative. For the physician,
it was a physical step back from the patient of approximately
25 cm, but in personal and professional terms it was a vast
move. No longer required to press an ear to the skin of the
patient, the physician moved away from the patient in a

physical and professional sense. The stethoscope became the trusted companion of the physician as it has become the symbol of healthcare today adorning the necks of health-care professionals. Personally, the physician was no longer required to place his face and head on the patient in order to hear faintly the heart and other organs. This contact required odd positioning and often embarrassing contact between the male physician and the female patient. With the stethoscope, the physician maintained a professionally superior position in relation to the patient. With the stethoscope as the intermediary, the physician trusted the instrument to convey truth in the form of clear sounds that could be interpreted to determine what was transpiring within the patient. The stethoscope took the place of the patient's description of what was transpiring internally. The sounds conveyed by the tool took the place of conversation. The actual sounds were more descriptive and more accurate than the vague commentary of the patient. In essence, the technology became the source of truth for the physician and the patient became secondary to the information obtained through the instrument.

This simple device should be viewed as the precursor to the technological foundation of scientific medicine in the 20th century. The history of healthcare is shaped by the simplest of items because healthcare is ultimately a personal interaction between physicians and patients that is repeated hundreds of thousands of times each day. The smallest process change replicated over and over transforms the whole. For healthcare, the act of examining a patient is the expression of a relationship between two people and the stethoscope transformed the experience of the relationship for the patient and the physician. This wooden tube exemplified the way in which new technology changed healthcare because it presaged the changes in the relationship between the physician and the patient that would occur with later technological developments. For the first time, the physician with a little training could actually know more about the patient than the patient knew simply by pressing a tube to the chest and listening. This new technology transformed the patient from a partner in healthcare, with a story that was vitally important to the physician's work, to the subject of care. The physician changed from a passive observer and interviewer to a healing professional who could explore the interior of the body and discover unseen truths useful in treating the patient.

In the 19th century, healthcare was defined as a conversation between a sick person and a physician as they worked together to try to understand what was happening to the sick person. The key elements of the care process were the words of the patient and the observations of the physician and whatever knowledge of natural medicine was available. In this exchange, the interaction between them expressed the fundamental nature of medicine and healthcare and the quality of care was the quality of the interaction. Even if the physician were unable to help to ease the suffering of the individual, the conversation they shared and the assistance provided were the basis for evaluating the quality of the care.

A shift in this ancient paradigm occurred with the medical technology revolution that began in the 19th century and gained speed throughout the 20th century. The most significant changes were the development of anesthesia, aseptic surgery, x-rays and laboratories. These new services and scientific methods required care to be delivered in its own unique production facility. This change moved the sick individual from the care of the family intimately aware of him or her as an individual to a facility, where they became one of many patients and the care process was controlled by strangers in uniforms. Hospitals grew in size and sophistication throughout the century and became in the end the palaces of the healthcare realm (Rosenberg 1987).

One aspect of the development of hospitals originating out of the 19th century was the concept of efficiency. Frederick W. Taylor in industry and Frank Gilbreth in hospitals and healthcare promoted the idea of efficiency through scientific management. By applying scientific methods such as conducting movement studies in the operating room (OR), a specialist could define the most efficient arrangement of instruments and movements by the surgeons to improve their surgical times. By properly organizing the hospital in such a way that leadership defines the work to be done and the way it is to be done and workers are trained to perform their work according to precise specifications, the entire organization can operate like an enormous scientific machine. These concepts were built into the way hospitals and their communities viewed their operations and the way that work and leadership should function in the early 20th century. These effects continue today in the operations of the most modern healthcare organizations (Gilbreth 1914; Taylor 1911).

Overseeing this evolving technological wonderland, the physician became a wizard of healing rather than a partner of the patient. As the American Medical Association raised the bar on physician education by standardizing the requirements for university and clinical training, the physician apprenticed in the new technology found in it the key to knowledge about the patient and to the ability to heal. Conversations with patients were less helpful than the laboratory reports of bacteria or the x-rays showing the fractured bones. In the operating room, the miraculous became routine as bodies were entered, repaired and returned to normal health without infections or the torturous pains of the past (Bonner 1995; Starr 1982).

The American Medical Association throughout the 20th century shaped the public perception of physicians and orchestrated the enhancement of the professional status of physicians. Medical boards supported by state statutes supervised licensure and monitored physician activities. Standards for education and clinical experience established by the AMA formed the basis for licensure by the states and licensure was required to order services for patients. Access to the local hospital and to its technology became essential to a successful career for physicians and membership on the local hospital medical staff with specific requirements for education and licensure served to create a powerful professional affiliation in the local health-care community.

As the technology proliferated, specialization became a hallmark of the medical professions. Specialists worked with companies to develop new technology and then used the technology to develop new specialties focused on more and more specific illnesses, organs and procedures. Specialization initially supported the goals of the American Medical Association in creating a distinctive view of physicians as a unique guild that should be shielded from the normal operations of markets and economics. However, as specialization expanded and costs increased, this created divergent professional groups that sapped the aggregate strength of the AMA and ultimately led to a diminished role in American healthcare (Starr 1982; Stevens 1998).

It is critically important to recognize that the understanding of the nature of healthcare as an industry in America in the 20th century grew out of the central role of technology and the professionalization of physicians. The growth of technology not only led to the development of enormous hospitals as the center of healthcare, but also created the belief by patients and healthcare itself that technology was commensurate with high quality. If a hospital had the latest medical technology and if a physician was trained in the latest procedures, they were able to deliver the highest quality care. For the patient and for the physician, technology and specialization served as the basis for healthcare quality in the 20th century. This understanding of medicine led to the proliferation of technology and specialization as hospitals and physicians promoted this vision of quality to the public. By defining the quality of healthcare as use of the latest technology and the best specialists, high utilization rates and high costs for healthcare services flowed as a natural result.

In other fields, advancement in technology and increased knowledge often led to higher productivity, higher quality and lower costs. American healthcare, as will be seen in the following chapters, did not experience these benefits because it was controlled by a profession unaffected by costs and committed to a view of quality based in high utilization of services and by a payment process in which the payer was not the recipient of the services. The system designed by the insurance companies and the providers and the employers and government provided access to technology and specialization as the path to higher quality until it finally ran out of money. This created the incentive for the redesign of healthcare through industrialization, as will be seen.

1.3 The Medical Record

When physicians began to treat their paying patients in the hospital rather than in their homes to take advantage of the latest technology and nursing services, the patient was no longer the sole responsibility of the physician, and the notes the physician wrote were no longer personal records of a private business. Within the hospital environment, the handwritten orders and notes of the physicians were the records of the care of patients and the directives that coordinated the services of a number of people, particularly nurses. This handwritten document served as the guide to the care of patients and solidified the role and control of the physician as the architect of the care process.

Handwritten orders were required for all the services to the patient, including admission to a specific unit and room in the hospital, type and quantity of food, ability of the patient to get up and move around, all the medications and treatments and so forth. All aspects of patient care were governed by the handwritten orders of the physician. The nursing staff used the documented physician orders as the basis for their care of the patient and ensured that the orders were followed precisely in order to achieve the results the physician desired for the patient. The power of the physician's pen literally dictated the services and care for the patient. Anyone who was involved in the care of the patient was required to consult the medical record and review all of the physician's orders and notes to know the status of the patient as determined by the physician and what was permitted for the patient.

For the hospital, the ability to provide services required nursing staff that could read and understand what the physician wrote and direct the various other services in complying with the orders. Interpretation of the handwritten orders constituted a major nursing skill since medication dosages and frequency could change a number of times in the course of a day.

Other services eventually had sections of the patient's medical record or chart in which they documented the services they provided. All of these records were handwritten and remained handwritten through most of the 20th century and were physically stored in the medical records department of the hospital. This was the official medical record of the patient and would be retrieved when the patient was readmitted to serve as an historical record of the patient's prior conditions and treatments.

As hospitals shifted their focus from charity care to patients able to pay for care and as the care of patients required the use of the new technology, the medical record became the basis for determining the costs and payments. During the era of charity care, the physicians communicated simple orders to the few staff members caring for the patients. The patient did not pay for the care and the costs to the hospital were the general expenditures to feed all the patients and to maintain the facility and simple staff. As new technology moved into the hospital and the costs of operations increased significantly, physicians and hospitals sought out paying patients. With paying patients, the physician still needed to communicate orders concerning the care of patients, but there was now a need to associate the orders of the physician with the services of the hospital in order to develop a bill for payment by the patient.

For hospitals, the physician's handwritten orders and notes became the medical record of the patient. By 1920, the American College of Surgeons (ACOS), as part of the Minimum Standards Program, required that "accurate and complete records are to be written for all patients, easily accessible with specific content" (ACOS 2006). The medical record increased in size and complexity over time, but remained essentially a hand-written record of the patient's care while in the hospital. The medical record became the official source of information about what the physician ordered for the patient while the patient was in the hospital. The physician's orders were the source of much of the costs associated with the care of the patient and the hospital business office worked to extract from the handwritten record all of the information that pertained to the patient's care in order to ensure that the patient was billed for what was provided according to the orders of the doctor.

For anyone involved in healthcare, the hardcopy, paper medical record remains an iconic image of the paradox of American healthcare. This voluminous, indecipherable, hand-written paper record shaped the work flows and the structure of hospital bureaucracy up to the present time for many organizations. It is doubtful that a more innocuous object with such a significant influence on healthcare could be imagined.

The medical record by its existence as a paper document that contained the handwritten orders and notes of the physician shaped the processes within the hospital throughout the 20th century. Nursing, pharmacy, laboratory, radiology and other departments established processes to access, absorb and implement these written orders to prevent errors resulting from misinterpretation of the writing. Physicians controlled the work of the hospital and the care of patients through these handwritten records.

Physicians structured their notes and their orders based on their medical training with only a slight nod to the attempts to standardize the written records in a particular hospital. Nursing, in particular, and other disciplines to a lesser degree were expected to learn to decipher the entries. By sustaining this method of documentation throughout the 20th century, hospitals and physician practices limited the availability of vital patient information to the physical record and the ability of staff to access and interpret the handwriting of the physician.

The breadth of the influence of the medical record in shaping hospitals and healthcare extends beyond the clinical care to the role these documents play in the assessment of the quality and efficiency of healthcare. In order to bill for care, hospitals and insurance companies use codes to describe the state of the patient and the services delivered by the hospital. Specially trained coders meticulously review the medical record after the patient has been discharged to identify diagnoses and health issues of the patient and the tests, procedures and services provided by the hospital. The coders document codes for each of these items. The manner in which the physician documented conclusions about the patient's care in notes remains today an essential element in determining the final bill and payment and quality of care. Coders spend hours reviewing individual charts to identify the key indicators required for specific codes associated with the patient's symptoms, diagnosis and procedures.

Though codes derived from the medical record were originally designed for payment, they became the basis for assessing the operations of the hospital and for evaluating the quality of the care that was delivered. Complications and other aspects of care derived from the notes documented by the physicians are aggregated and analyzed to assess the quality of the care delivered by the hospital. Based on these codes, hospitals are publicly rated and compared. To imagine that a document that carries so much weight in the overall revenue of healthcare organizations and in healthcare as an industry is handwritten on paper in cursive by physicians is to begin to see why the introduction of electronic information systems was so traumatic to physicians and required massive reengineering for healthcare organizations.

Given this history and the influence of the paper medical record in shaping hospital processes, it is not surprising that physicians in particular and hospitals and American healthcare in general were slow to embrace electronic medical records and absolutely shocked by the encounter when it finally occurred. Certain aspects of healthcare, such as the financial and business office operations, eased into the electronic age through the acquisition of adding machines that made it easier to get to the bottom line. The calculator was a fancy adding machine that was faster and easier to use. Finally, the arrival of the computer system with an electronic accounting package made it even easier to calculate the income and the expenses. For accounting and finance, the computer was a welcome companion whose coming had been long predicted in each step of the calculating technology (Howell 1995).

On the clinical side, computers appeared in isolated areas of the hospital to perform specific tasks. Early mainframe computers made it possible for the laboratory and other subsections of hospital operations to track tests and specimens and to report results. As these early computers became cheaper and smaller and more sophisticated and as new programs specific to particular sections of the hospital developed, they proliferated but remained islands of data. As a constant point of reference, providing the information to the physician was all that was required for the care of the patient. The islands of information in separate computers remained through most of the 20th century. With the advent of the Internet and the realization that connecting these islands of information made them more useful, healthcare slowly implemented information systems.

With the emergence of the Internet and the concept of connectivity between computers, the physician and the hospital were forced to adapt to the new technology. The handwritten medical record served as a cornerstone of the work flow of the craftsman physician until the early 21st century and remains as one of the last visible signs of physician control over patient care. It is not surprising that this document was a significant impediment to the earlier expansion of electronic information systems into hospital clinical processes. Physicians absolutely resisted the intrusion of the computer into the care process on several levels (IOM [Institute of Medicine] 2001, 2012).

Initially, the use of computers changed the work flow for the physicians. Confident in methods used throughout their careers, physicians sought to retain the handwritten record as a familiar and trusted method for controlling hospital processes and directing the care of patients. Secondly, the act of typing on a computer represented a threat to the visible status of the physician within the hospital culture. Typing had always been associated with clerical activities. For physicians, this act symbolized a change in their role and status. Thirdly, information systems in hospitals created standardized processes of care and documentation. For physicians, the standardization of care represented another attempt to alter their status in the care process. If the computer established the care of the patient, what was the function of the physician? The act of practicing medicine and delivering care became a mouse click that anyone could do. Finally, as sophisticated computer systems intruded into the life of the hospital, information became available to anyone with access to the system. The handwritten notes of the physician were no longer the source of truth and point of reference for knowledge about the patient. The physician's input into the system became just one more piece of data in the overall record of the patient's care and everyone had the ability to review all the data and to be an active participant in designing the care of the patient.

Slowly, enterprise systems developed in which information from multiple areas could be stored in centralized servers and accessed through computers throughout the hospital. Though this was arduous and required delicate diplomacy between the various specialties, progress was made and more disciplines had real-time access to information about patients and could communicate electronically in real time with each other. This opened the way for hospitals to link departments and services and for hospitals to link with other hospitals and agencies (DHHS 2012).

The handwritten record of patient care provides a meaningful illustration of a profound reality of the evolution of healthcare in the 20th century. Each patient's record was essentially the work of a craftsman physician who exercised immense control. In reflecting back on the history of this document within the context of the development of American history, the influence of the paper, handwritten medical record in shaping the healthcare industry cannot be overestimated. As a force within healthcare, it shaped the daily routines of care and served as a formidable barrier to innovation and change. In its solidity as a single document and the central repository for all the care associated with the patient, it exerted a profound gravitational pull on all processes and activities associated with the patient from the initial encounter to the charges to the assessment of care following discharge.

The pervasive influence of the paper medical record in shaping American healthcare became clear as hospitals and physicians struggled to absorb the new computer technology and Internet connectivity. Recent changes at the national level that are creating changes at the local level that will encourage consideration of industrialization involve the American Recovery and Reinvestment Act (ARRA) funds for health information system implementation in hospitals. Hospitals across America are working to meet the requirements for the funding to support healthcare information technology in the form of electronic medical records. This initiative affects the basic work flows and organizational structures designed in the 20th century to manage the paper medical records, because it requires hospitals and physician practices to implement and use electronic medical records rather than handwritten records (ARRA 2009).

In light of the role of the paper medical record in hospitals and other healthcare organizations, it is clear that this change will not be easily absorbed or easily dismissed. For the clinical staff of the hospital, the way they engage with patients and the ways that they document their observations and activities must change significantly to accommodate the use of computers and electronic documentation. The devices must be brought to the patient rooms or be in the rooms. The patient and clinician must find a way to communicate with each other as the computer sits between them as an intermediate element in their interactions. For the patients and clinical staff, the documentation set up in the computer assumes a greater role in structuring their interactions than previously when the interaction involved the clinician's own processes and method of documentation. The electronic record structures the interaction and requires responses.

The intrusion of the electronic record into the work flow of the physician also creates a challenge in terms of the perception of the role of the physician. Using a keyboard and typing orders and notes carries the connotation of clerical work, which is difficult for physicians to accept. The electronic record contains order sets and clinical support documentation designed to guide the physician's orders and examination. This seems to imply certain deficits on the part of the physician.

The difficulty of this change and the resistance inherent in the system and the profound changes required to bring electronic information systems into healthcare illustrate the central role of the medical record in the life of American healthcare. As will be discussed later, the influence of healthcare information technology and the connectivity of information systems in the 21st century form the basis for the emergence of new work flows and processes that are as transformative in shaping the future of American healthcare as the original medical record was in shaping its past.

1.4 The Money

As new technology, the new professional status of physicians and the emergence of the hospital as the factory of healing transformed the delivery of American healthcare, payment became a problem. It was in this area that the true American entrepreneurial spirit appeared and reshaped a private crafts-man business based on a simple exchange of money or trade for services into one of the most sophisticated and unintelli-gible financial structures ever imagined to support one of the largest industries ever created.

As we have seen, healthcare in America began as a craftsman-based private business in which individuals paid for services and wealthy benefactors supported charity care for the poor. These systems for paying for the minimal health-care services available in the 19th century were relatively simple and very familiar to patients. The payment process reflected the nature of these exchanges. Physicians came to the home and delivered services and received payment. The destitute and ill went to the charity hospitals and received care paid for by the wealthy. These simple, straightforward payment processes clearly reflected the values of society in the respon-sibility of the individual or family to pay for healthcare and the requirement that the wealthy share their abundance with the downtrodden as Christian charity and to prevent dead bodies from lying in the streets (Rosenberg 1987; Starr 1982).

When entrepreneurial physicians and hospital benefactors sought new sources of revenue to pay for the new technology they acquired, wealthy and middle-class patients represented the most logical source for new funds. Having received care in the comfort and privacy of their homes for centuries, how-ever, patients with the ability to pay for care did not simply show up at the local hospital and demand access. Going to a hospital required a complete reorientation for the pillars of society. They viewed these establishments as necessary but not a fitting environment for anyone not required by circum-stances to seek care there.

It took a new relationship between physicians and hospi-tals to create a new healthcare business model to persuade potential patients to leave their homes and to come to a place reserved previously for the outcasts in society. The physicians in the role of salesmen and often managers and the hospitals in the role of a hotel with benefits created a new entrepreneurial industry of healthcare services. This shift represented a move from the individual physician delivering services for payment in the home of patients to a production facility in which the hospital sought to finance its operations from the payments of patients. This new model changed the relationship between physicians and hospitals. Previously, physicians sought the right to attend to patients admitted to the hospital as a way to gain skills and build a reputation in the community and they donated their services. The wealthy benefactors paying the bills for the local hospital controlled admissions and managed the access of physicians to the patients in the hospital. With the need for paying patients to support the hospital, physicians as the salesmen of healthcare gained a significant amount of control over the local hospital and its services (Rosenberg 1987; Starr 1982).

As the hospitals and physicians began to view the local community as a market for hospitals' services and sought to expand their reach into this market, the message to patients was that the hospital and its physicians offered the benefits of the new science of medicine. The acquisition of technology as well as the quality of rooms and nursing service became important in attracting enough paying patients to maintain a modern facility with the latest equipment. To ease the transition of wealthy patrons from home to hospitals, the comforts of home were brought to the hospital. Private suites with rooms for servants away from the charity care areas in the hospital offered familiar comforts to the wealthy. Richly appointed furnishings and the personal attention of private-duty nurses and the patient's personal physician created a new status for hospital services (Howell 1995; Rosenberg 1987; Starr 1982).

The clear benefits of the new scientific medicine impressed society. Patients did not suffer and die from infections as a routine part of surgical care. Nurses created a professional and well-structured hospital environment that satisfied the needs and expectations of middle-class American patients. Hospital operations became more departmental and bureaucratic to manage the new services and to support the new technology required to deliver care. The new expenses associated with the facilities and services required hospitals to create new finance departments and accounting expertise to manage the new financial operations. Physicians brought more paying patients to the hospital and struggled with their growing patient population and the requirement that they donate their services to the other patients in the hospital. The new business of healthcare redesigned itself to attract and care for paying patients, and this new business depended on these paying patients (Starr 1982; Rosenberg 1987; Howell 1995).

The Great Depression of the 1920s and 1930s offered hospitals the opportunity to see a world in which patients desired but could not pay for services. Hospitals as the new healthcare production facility could no longer survive on the donations of the wealthy but required a continuous revenue stream from paying patients. As this revenue stream dried up during the Depression, hospitals suffered from empty rooms not because patients did not want care but rather because they could no longer afford care.

American entrepreneurial spirit rescued healthcare with the idea of prepayments for hospital services before they were needed to guarantee availability of services in the event of illness or injury. The introduction of prepayment for hospital services offered a new revenue stream to hospitals to sustain their operations even when patients were not in the hospital. Healthy people began to prepay for hospital services the same way they prepaid for burial services to ensure that they had the service not if but when they needed it. This payment model supported the view that the use of hospital services was anticipated as a normal part of healthcare and that prepayment was an acceptable way to obtain this care (Thomasson 2003).

The move from the prepayment of hospital services to healthcare insurance represented a reasonable progression also supported by the American entrepreneurial drive. World War II, like the Great Depression, created a new situation in American life. The drain of labor into the military left American manufacturing short of workers. With wages frozen, other ways to attract workers were needed and companies turned to healthcare as an incentive. The cost of hospital care was not overly burdensome to employers and was attractive to potential employees. The government supported healthcare as a benefit with favorable tax treatment for businesses and individuals, and this worked for organized labor (Rosenberg 1987; Thomasson 2003; Starr 2011).

During and after World War II, employer-sponsored hospital insurance established a new business model for healthcare in which the mechanism for the payment of healthcare services operated through insurance companies. Individuals and families received hospital insurance coverage as a benefit of employment and did not directly pay for hospital care or have to worry about shopping for services they could afford. It was all worked out between the hospital, the insurer, and the employer (Rosenberg 1987; Thomasson 2003; Starr 2011).

This new financing model promoted the use of the local hospital and supported its role as the source of healthcare services. Physicians routinely ordered tests and services for their patients through the local hospital, where they admitted patients and conducted rounds daily on their hospitalized patients. The hospital had all the tests and technology physicians needed, and patients desired the best treatment. Payment was guaranteed by the insurance company. Patients came to assume they would receive healthcare at the local hospital and expected that any sickness or illness beyond the very simple would receive hospital care. Hospitals and healthcare technology companies promoted the use of the hospital as the best place for care and constantly marketed the acquisition of new technology and new services. For hospitals and physicians, the only challenge was attracting patients to their hospital. Advertising new technology and high-quality facilities became a part of the way in which the healthcare delivery system increased revenues.

Insurance became the standard method of payment for Americans receiving healthcare services. The poor continued to be served through charity care at the local hospital and the working population benefitted from employer-sponsored healthcare insurance. The elderly, however, who no longer worked, had no access to healthcare services and this created a tremendous burden on families at the same time that they enjoyed healthcare insurance for themselves. The American Medical Association successfully fought every effort by politicians to create a national hospital insurance plan through most of the 20th century, but when healthcare for the elderly appeared in the early 1960s as a proposal, Congress passed it. Medicare provided cost-based hospital and physician coverage for the last remaining uninsured populations in the country by providing healthcare insurance for anyone over age 65 and making provisions for the poor and disabled through Medicaid. Hospitals and physicians enjoyed the benefits of employer-sponsored insurance for workers and federally supported healthcare for the elderly and poor. These new healthcare insurance programs fueled competition between hospitals, which sought to obtain the best technology and specialist physicians in order to attract more patients. With insurance paying the bills, the more patients a hospital could serve the more revenue to cover costs and expansion it would generate (Thomasson 2003; Starr 2011).

As hospitals competed for larger shares of the patient market, medical technology companies sought to gain market for their technology. New technology was presented as offering hospitals advantages for their patients and as incentives to attract physicians. The expansion of the market to the elderly added fuel to the fire of technological development and expanded hospital utilization. All of this was consistent with the American view of technology, physicians and hospitals as the sources of health. During the postwar expansion, the cost was built into the employer and government payment systems, and individuals and families viewed hospital insurance coverage as a part of their work life and Medicare as part of their retirement.

Beginning in the 1950s, construction of hospitals across the country made access to modern healthcare services a reality even in rural areas. Physicians moved out of the cities to small towns as local hospitals provided the technology and services they needed to care for patients. Most people had some form of health insurance to pay for hospital care and physician services. Cost-based government funding and the growth of commercial insurance fueled the research and development efforts of pharmaceutical and medical technology industries. Physician specialization increased as the technology and options for care expanded. The country as a whole viewed the growth of healthcare services as a major contributor to the quality of life in America (Stevens 1999).

The party lasted until the bill came due and the federal government experienced "sticker shock."

Within a decade of the passage of Medicare, the rapid growth in costs led to calls for changes. The government began to address the cost issue by developing a plan for coding diagnoses; rather than a straight cost-based reimbursement, the hospital would receive a diagnosis-related payment set by Medicare to cover the costs of care. Over the years, the prospective payment program gradually reduced the rate of payment for covered diagnoses.

American manufacturing and businesses enjoyed a tremendous burst of productivity following World War II as the world struggled to recover from the destruction while America produced the materials. American production facilities were unaffected by the war and rapidly made the transition from war to peacetime production to provide goods for the reconstruction. By the 1970s, however, the world had recovered and competition increased. American manufacturing built on quantity rather than quality began to see market share declines and growth slowing. The rising costs of healthcare insurance premiums for employees put pressure on the business's bottom line and forced a reconsideration of healthcare insurance as an employee benefit.

By the end of the 20th century, the cost of healthcare had grown from a concern to a perceived threat to the economic viability of the United States. Though there were many attempts to reduce the rate of hospital and physician price increases that led to higher insurance premium increases, no method was successful. American healthcare design required hospital-based, technology-driven, specialized healthcare as a basic structure. With this structure, the payment processes for healthcare reflected the unique nature of America that values individuality, entrepreneurial spirit and personal responsibility. The move to an all-insurance-based payment process operating through employers and the government functioned well through most of the century and fit the AMA view of the unique professional role of the physician and the expansion of hospitals as the delivery system for healthcare that supported the development of technology-based acute care. In all of these areas, there was no mechanism designed to limit the cost of care. Like manufacturing after World War II, America designed a system to produce great quantities of healthcare but did not design it to be efficient or necessarily effective. This approach created the most expensive healthcare production system in the world (Thomasson 2003; Starr 2011).

The Patient Protection and Affordable Care Act (PPACA) of 2010–2014 provided some adjustments, but the basic formula of commercial and governmental insurance remained in place. In the PPACA, Medicare is required to pursue value rather than volume and to develop payments based on performance.

For the local hospital, Medicare has often been a lower payer but has always been a consistent payer. With the development of these new initiatives, the ability of the hospital to maintain a reasonable margin hinges on the delivery of care that meets all the requirements established by Medicare (Office of Legislative Counsel 2010).

As the largest payer, Medicare sets the pattern for all payers and the commercial insurers are also looking to develop payment processes that vary depending on the quality of the care.

In addition to the efforts by Medicare to promote quality as basis for payment, employers are implementing insurance plans for their employees that require significant participation by the employees in paying for care before the insurance coverage begins. These high-deductible plans are designed to encourage patients to search for better healthcare values because they will be using their own funds to pay for care. They also put the hospital and other providers at risk if patients are not able to cover their deductibles (Galbraith et al. 2011).

The method for reducing the rate of cost increases envisioned by the PPACA focused on requiring providers— hospitals and physicians—to produce healthcare services at higher quality to limit payments for poor quality. Hospitals and physicians viewed utilization of healthcare services as the equivalent of good healthcare. This approach has been shown to increase costs without improving the well-being of patients (IOM 2012, 2013). With cost as the main driver, the question of quality has become a central focus of the efforts of government and employers to find a solution to paying for healthcare. If more care is not better care, then what is the measure of healthcare? If technology and specialization are not the guarantees of the quality of care, is there another way to determine the amount and the kind of care needed in order to achieve the efficient delivery of high-quality healthcare?

Chapter 2

Healthcare Quality History

2.1 Introduction

Talking about healthcare quality is a very 21st century concept. For most of the 20th century, the quality of healthcare was assumed to be as good as the provider. As a craftsman business, quality meant a credentialed physician with the appropriate degrees and licenses and a hospital equipped with the best technology and professional nursing staff. These essentials offered the best guarantee of good quality care. Given this historic perspective, the debate of the nature of healthcare quality today offers a very different perspective than was historically the case.

Healthcare quality today emerged out of the convergence of two historic streams: quality care from within healthcare and quality defined by industry. The first stream grew out of the 20th century professionalization of medicine and the technological developments that improved care and the survival of patients. As hospitals created new operating rooms and laboratories and nursing services, these epitomized the latest developments in healthcare. To offer these services in a well-structured, organized manner represented the highest possible quality of care.

A second historical stream began in the last quarter of the 20th century as American industry responded to a competitive challenge from Japan and other countries. These countries recovered their productivity following World War II and created a new standard of quality and efficiency that exceeded that of American businesses. The quantity-based, mass production industrial model that won World War II struggled to respond to this new challenge. Eventually, after significant disruption and contraction, American industry developed new approaches to quality to reduce costs and waste and became competitive once again.

These two streams converged in the last decades of the 20th century to form the transformative industrialization that has begun to reshape American healthcare today. As healthcare costs increased in the 20th century and consumers conditioned to new industrial levels of quality and safety raised questions about healthcare results, the solution appeared to be the introduction of mass production quality concepts and techniques into healthcare. Through this process, industrialized quality in the form of Lean and Six Sigma and other methodologies became a transformative force in healthcare.

This chapter introduces a surprising development in the history of healthcare that was not anticipated. With the physician, the hospital and the patients as the three key components of healthcare, the stool seemed quite sturdy. Surprisingly, however, in subtle ways at first and then in a building crescendo, the quality of the care delivered to patients began to be questioned and this threatened the entire structure. The next section describes the initial efforts to ensure the quality of healthcare in the early 20th century. Inspection to assure that the bare essentials were met remained the method for quality assurance in healthcare through most of the century. The piece of paper from the university that the physician presented as his credentials and the hospital policy describing the basic requirements for a medical record were the standard signs of quality in healthcare during this period. Section 2.3, "Quality from outside Healthcare," describes how the industrial quality revolution ignited a fire in healthcare and the healthcare edifice carefully constructed and preserved during the 20th century began to crumble. Industrial mass production quality in the form of process improvement, statistical process control, and Lean and Six Sigma was called upon to transform healthcare by the government and the payers as the quest for cost controls found no other solution.

2.2 Quality from within Healthcare

It is important to understand that healthcare quality in early America was more a question of access to care than the delivery of good care. If you had no access to care, there really was no question about its quality. Physicians were rare. Healthcare for most of America in the early days was the person in town with the most experience setting bones or delivering babies or knowledge about local herbs who provided advice when someone was sick. Families did the best that they could with the resources they had. Midwives or wise older women were often the healthcare providers in their villages.

Physicians trained in Europe practiced in the large cities in colonial America. To ask a physician with European training about the quality of the care he provided would have been a serious breach of etiquette. Quality was assumed because the physician had a degree. Since there were very few people with those credentials, there were very few who could question the care provided by the physician. If educated in Europe and trained in the classics of medicine, the physician was prepared to deliver care or at least to describe the patient's illness in the correct Latin terms. The outcome for the patient was less of a concern for the well-educated physicians of the 18th century than properly classifying the disease. Due to the limited rcsources available for actually treating illnesses, accurately identifying the disease and describing the prognosis were the extent of the physician's capability (Starr 1982; Bonner 1995).

Improvements in care in the 19th century surprisingly emerged out of the wars in Europe, the Crimea and in America. Generating lots of patients for physicians and surgeons, the wars served as catalysts for actual improvements in patient care that eventually made their way into civilian circles. In the Crimea, Florence Nightingale and her nurses found large numbers of sick and injured soldiers dying from the poor conditions in the hospitals more than from their injuries. She and her nurses established new standards to improve the care and tracked the effects of the changes using charts of mortality rates of the patients. Taking what she learned back to England, Nightingale created the fundamentals for professional nursing care within hospitals (Rosenberg 1987).

In the American Civil War in the 1860s, the Army field hospitals were slowly transformed into effective and efficient places for caring for wounded soldiers. The hundreds of thousands of soldiers who were treated in these hospitals reported on their experiences when they returned home. The efficiency and cleanliness and quality of the care in the field hospitals made an impression that promoted a more positive view of hospitals and encouraged civilian patients to consider going to hospitals for care (Rosenberg 1987).

As the wars brought changes to patient care, a significant influence on the definition of quality in medicine in America was the American Medical Association (AMA). Founded in 1847, the AMA established a Committee on Medical Education to create standards for preliminary medical education and for the MD degree. In its early days, the association published information about nostrums or medications that were not proven to work and identified practices that were contrary to accepted scientific medical practices. This was part of the struggle between scientific, university-based medical schools and the naturalistic approaches of homeopathic and naturopathic care. These publications were initially the only source of information available on these topics (Starr 1982).

In 1913, the AMA used funding from the Andrew Carnegie Foundation to finance a review of medical schools across the country conducted by Abraham Flexner. Flexner, knowledge-able of the Johns Hopkins University approach to medical education in which university training was combined with clinical time in hospitals, determined that the majority of proprietary schools in operation at the time were not equipped or staffed to properly train physicians and were not associated with universities or hospitals. Following his report, he worked with the Rockefeller Foundation to provide funds to schools modeled after Hopkins. Many of the proprietary schools that were unable to meet the standards closed, as did schools unaligned with universities. The education of physicians migrated to medical schools affiliated with universities and hospitals where the training was based on standardized views of scientific medicine. With these changes, the cost of medical education increased more than many could afford. For those who could afford the education, the decline in the number of physicians increased their status and their ability to earn a good rate of pay (Starr 1982; Bonner 1995).

As medical education became standardized and surgery became a more common aspect of care, an early pioneer in improving surgical care, Ernest A. Codman at Massachusetts General Hospital (MGH), promoted the concept of assessing the quality of care by following the outcomes of surgical patients or the "end results." He recommended surgeons follow their patients for a year after surgery. Though a graduate of Harvard, he was removed from the medical staff of Massachusetts General Hospital because of his ardent commitment to this idea for assessing quality (Rosenberg 1987).

Codman's very modern recommendation of analyzing outcomes was rejected, but he influenced the process of healthcare quality nonetheless through his appointment in 1910 to a new Committee on Hospital Standardization created by the American College of Surgeons (ACOS). Codman recognized the value of patient medical records in assessing the quality of care and advocated for including patient medical records in the American College of Surgeons' Hospital Standardization Program's five specific standards that were to be used to survey hospitals. The five "minimum standards" of the Hospital Standardization Program reflected the healthcare quality standards of the time and continue to play an important role in healthcare quality today in expanded forms. They established the process of measuring quality by inspecting hospitals to ensure that certain structures, policies and services were present.

The first three standards require the hospital medical staff—those physicians and surgeons privileged to practice at the hospital—to define themselves as a group that includes in its membership only graduates of medical schools who are licensed and to create rules, regulations and policies to govern professional work. The final two standards set forth the essentials required of the hospital, specifically to maintain and make accessible accurate and complete medical records on all patients and to provide clinical laboratory and x-ray services (ACOS 2006).

In 1951 the Joint Commission on Accreditation of Hospitals, created by merging the American College of Surgeons' Hospital Standardization Program with similar programs run by the American College of Physicians, the American Hospital Association, the American Medical Association and the Canadian Medical Association took over inspection of hospitals. In 1987, it was renamed the Joint Commission on Accreditation of Healthcare Organizations and later was named the Joint Commission. The principal method for improving quality in healthcare was the triennial survey by the Joint Commission on Accreditation of Hospitals. The Joint Commission, however, did not address quality assurance beyond simple requirements until the 1970s (Sollecito and Johnson 2013).

In 1966, Dr. Avedi Donabedian published his review of literature of health services research as it appeared through the 1950s and early 1960s in a paper titled, "Evaluating the Quality of Medical Care." He identified the need for quality to be based on structure, process and outcomes of healthcare. Structure referred to all the resources available for the delivery of healthcare services. Process referred to all the actual measures of care (medication administration, etc.). Outcomes referred to results of care. Donabedian's approach to healthcare quality influenced many early efforts to understand and improve the actual work of healthcare (Donabedian 1980; Sollecito and Johnson 2013).

With the passage of the law creating Medicare and Medicaid in 1965, government-funded healthcare became a reality. The "conditions of participation" for hospitals to be permitted by the government to take care of Medicare patients established standards for care. Hospitals could choose to be surveyed by Medicare to ensure that they complied with the conditions of participation or by the Joint Commission. As with other programs in healthcare, inspection, whether by Medicare or by the Joint Commission, continued to be the primary way in which hospital quality was evaluated. The conditions of participation did not have provisions for actually assessing quality of care, other than the requirement for the medical staff to evaluate cases, until after the 1980s (Lohr 1990).

Considering the current low status of inspection by agencies as a means for assessing quality in healthcare, it may seem counterintuitive to the modern healthcare professional that this was the best that healthcare could do officially in the 20th century. This method of assessing quality actually refers to the clinical quality rather than to operational quality. Quality in other areas of the hospital such as the laundry, food service, housekeeping and many other activities was based on the actual quality produced. Complaints or poor performance in these areas could be addressed by managers or supervisors.

Why was clinical quality—the quality of care provided by the professionals—so problematic? Beginning with the physicians, the issue focused on the prerogatives of professionals and the responsibility of the medical staff that formed the physician's peer group. With education completed and license in hand, physicians as independent practitioners applied for privileges at hospitals. The medical staff and board of the hospital granted those privileges or denied them. Once a physician was a member of the medical staff, the relationships with other physicians became very important in maintaining that membership. In many cases, physicians on the medical staff could be colleagues or competitors.

Evaluating the quality of another physician's medical practice was and is today a very delicate matter. As craftsmen, physicians are regarded as the experts. Physicians consider only someone of comparable training and experience a peer and able to offer credible insight into whether a clinical situation was addressed appropriately. Even in litigation, it is the opinions of experts for both the plaintiff and the defendant that are presented as establishing whether care was properly delivered. Since the reputation of a physician is the foundation of his or her livelihood, suggesting that a peer physician delivered poor care could be seen as an attempt to eliminate a competitor or could lead to the alienation of a colleague. Due to the democratic nature of medical staff proceedings, physicians would be hesitant to point out poor skills in other physicians since they might need their support in the future.

Beyond the relationships with other physicians, judging the outcomes of care remains a tricky business. The complexity of human physiology and pathology and the ability of patients to deviate from the advice of their physicians make the prospect of assigning blame for poor outcomes problematic. Advice that does not come out of the established channels of trusted colleagues may not be well accepted. Dr. Codman's situation, in which his peers at MGH took offense at the idea of evaluating the quality of surgery by following the outcomes of patients for an extended period, may provide useful insights into the difficulty that healthcare has had with measuring and improving clinical quality.

2.3 Quality from outside Healthcare

The notion that quality is expensive is reasonable when you are talking to an individual craftsman. If you want high-quality furniture, clothing or any other goods, they cost more than goods of lesser quality. This makes sense when the goods are produced by the individual craftsman, because the quality is based on a number of factors that are routinely in short supply. The skill of the individual requires time to develop and there are not many craftsmen who have the appropriate skill level. The time to actually make a high-quality product is greater because the skill of the craftsman is expressed in intricate, precise work. This reduces the number of products the craftsman can make. The quality is derived from the materials and the best materials are almost always in short supply. Simple economics dictate that the best materials cost more due to demand exceeding supply. For the individual craftsman, then, high-quality goods require more training, more time to create and materials that are more costly. It makes perfect sense, therefore, that customers should pay more for quality.

Mass production resulting from the industrial revolutions of the 18th and 19th centuries changed the quality equation in a significant way. With water, steam and electrical power, interchangeable parts and machinery, the craftsman's work moved from the individual to thousands of machines that quickly produced large quantities of goods. The machinery replicated the work of the craftsman and the new sources of power replaced part of the human labor. With machine-driven production, large numbers of items could be manufactured more rapidly.

Henry Ford's development of the moving assembly line in the early 20th century accelerated complex product creation.

Workers remained in place and performed simple processes of assembling interchangeable parts on a continuously moving conveyor belt. Through these and other techniques, the mass production of goods at relatively consistent levels of quality made more products of higher quality available at lower costs.

Mass production revolutionized production of goods and significantly increased the goods available for consumption. Large quantities of products became available to many more people at lower costs than were possible for individual craftsmen. These developments changed the relationship between cost and quality in terms of the actual cost required to make a product. However, the speed at which raw materials could be converted into finished products increased the potential for significant costs due to malfunctions in the processes that produced defective products.

Initially, inspection at the end of the manufacturing process and the discarding of defective parts maintained quality for the people purchasing the finished goods. As long as enough products could be produced to cover the costs of the discarded goods, manufacturing moved forward. As the speed of production increased and final products required multiple parts to be assembled, discarding defective products at the end of the line became much more costly. Finding a way to maintain quality without discarding large quantities of products became an important consideration.

Beginning in the 19th century, American gun makers started measuring manufactured parts rather than estimating the dimensions. This reduced the number of parts that were rejected at the time of final assembly of the gun. By increasing the precision of the inspection through actual measurement, manufacturing improved. To prevent losses, companies needed to be able to identify production problems and product defects as soon as they occurred in the manufacturing process so that they did not result in large numbers of discarded parts with defects (Ellis and Whittington 1993).

In 1924 at the Western Electric Hawthorne plant, Walter Shewhart recognized the problems associated with inspection in mass production and he developed the concepts of statistical process control based on evaluating samples from the production line. Shewhart demonstrated that defective parts could be identified during the manufacturing process and the process problems corrected. This prevented the creation of large quantities of defective parts that had to be discarded at the end of the production line. It also made it possible to assess quality for large quantities of goods by looking at only a sample rather than inspecting every part. In his 1931 book, *Economic Control of Quality of Manufactured Product*, Shewhart created the first statistical control charts for manufacturing processes that involved statistical sampling procedures.

Reconstruction of Japan after World War II included bringing Japanese industry back from the devastating destruction of the war. To aid in this effort, W. Edwards Deming, Joseph Juran and others were asked to assist the Japanese in improving the quality of their products. Deming, who had worked closely with Shewhart, encouraged the Japanese to focus on continuously improving the processes of production rather than inspecting products and discarding poor quality at the end. He recommended that they listen to their customers and include their suppliers in the improvement of their processes (Berwick, Godfrey and Rossner 1990).

The Great Depression of the 1930s idled much of the American workforce. With the start of World War II, American industry and American workers were called upon to produce the weapons and materials to win a war. By the end of the war, America had created the great engine of American mass production and turned its attention to consumer goods for a world in reconstruction. American industry produced the goods that the world needed and in the process created a new prosperity for American workers.

In the 1980s, however, manufacturing in America suddenly became aware of changes occurring inside and outside the country. The quality training of the 1950s by Deming and Juran and the elimination of waste and pursuit of perfection promoted at Toyota in the 1970s by Taiichi Ohno were paying off as Japan's newly rebuilt productive capability produced high-quality goods at lower prices. From within America, Motorola responded to their own poor quality by applying the work of Shewhart and other quality leaders to reduce the variation in production processes as the basis for improving quality. Bill Smith's efforts at Motorola resulted in the creation of the quality management program referred to as "Six Sigma" due to the statistical goal of 3.4 defects per million opportunities. Built from a combination of quality concepts and techniques, Six Sigma debuted around the country as Motorola shared its efforts as a result of winning the 1988 Malcolm Baldrige National Quality Award. In the hands of GE and other companies, Six Sigma reduced cost by reducing defects to almost zero and transformed manufacturing processes (Berwick, Godfrey and Roessner 1990).

As American manufacturing woke up to the realization that quality was the path to the future and Japan and Motorola's quality initiatives in the 1980s were leading the way, individuals working to improve American healthcare stumbled into it as well. Paul Batalden, MD, attended a W. Edwards Deming seminar in the early 1980s and ultimately contributed to Deming's book, *Out of the Crisis*. Batalden was so convinced of the validity of Deming's approach that he convinced the CEO of Hospital Corporation of America (HCA), a large, for-profit hospital company, to embrace it. Batalden worked at HCA to develop and present training in Deming's concepts and the new industrial quality techniques for thousands of future healthcare leaders (Kenney 2008).

Batalden met Donald Berwick, MD, and introduced him to Deming's concept and encouraged him to attend a Deming conference. After a rocky start, Berwick was also persuaded.

Berwick and Batalden and others ultimately founded the
Institute for Healthcare Improvement to promote industrial
quality improvement in healthcare (Kenney 2008).

The unique nature of American healthcare makes it resistant to new concepts that originate outside the familiar clinical
training channels and it was not different for the introduction
of mass production quality improvement into healthcare.
This was illustrated by the National Demonstration Project
on Quality Improvement in Healthcare conducted in 1987.
Over 20 healthcare organizations agreed to participate in
an 8-month study of the applicability of industrial quality
improvement methods in healthcare. They were supported by
a number of large corporations. The end result was mixed and
healthcare did not jump on the industrial quality improvement
train (Berwick et al. 1990).

In the 1990s, however, reports began to appear that all
was not well in healthcare. Perhaps the most dramatic and,
at the time, controversial were the 1999 Institute of Medicine
report, *To Err Is Human: Building a Safer Health System,* and
the follow-up report in 2001, *Crossing the Quality Chasm.*
These opened to public gaze the hidden errors and deaths
in healthcare from the processes of care and challenged
American healthcare to build a future on quality improvement. Along with Lucian Leape, MD, Berwick, Batalden and
others sounded the alarm that people were dying because
of the poor quality of American healthcare, but healthcare's
resistance to change continued even as the evidence of serious
problems increased.

Perhaps even more significant in opening the processes of
healthcare to outside review and creating a channel for the
introduction of industrial quality was the growing consensus
that America could not sustain the rising cost of healthcare.
Beginning in the 1970s, efforts were initiated to reduce the
rate of the increases in healthcare costs. Health management
organizations (HMO) sought to control costs by controlling the
utilization of services. The government created professional

service review organizations to evaluate utilization of services and the prospective payment system to establish reimbursement rates for specific diagnoses. The failure of these and other approaches to successfully reduce increases in healthcare spending in the 1980s and 1990s fueled growing governmental and employer frustration with healthcare as an industry (IOM 2012).

Despite the seemingly recalcitrant posture of American hospitals and physicians on the questions of quality and cost, efforts were being made to understand the sources of costs and variations in quality in American healthcare. In 1996, the Dartmouth Atlas of Healthcare was one of the first to point out variations in care and spending based on Medicare data on a national basis. The Joint Commission on Accreditation of Healthcare Organizations (JCAHO) recognized the growing demand for data on healthcare performance and launched the ORYX initiative in 1997. Accredited healthcare organizations were required to submit performance data on several diagnoses to JCAHO as a way to move beyond triennial inspection surveys to data-driven, continuous performance processes. This represented one of the first efforts on a national scale to compare data on hospital clinical performance. The Centers for Medicare and Medicaid Services (CMS) began to make subtle moves to bring about change. In 2005, the Medicare website, Hospital Compare, went public with data on seventeen processes of care drawing from data based on the JCAHO ORYX initiative. CMS added patient satisfaction data in 2008 as well as comparison sites for dialysis services, home health and nursing homes.

The Institute of Medicine (IOM) brought forth another report on quality and costs in healthcare in 2012 with the report, *Best Care at Lower Cost.* In this report, the IOM focused on the successes of manufacturing and service industries in improving quality and reducing costs and the failures of healthcare to achieve similar results. In this report, the IOM shifted the debate from what healthcare should do to the reality of the world of consumers of healthcare. Consumers measure healthcare not against itself but rather against the best in the marketplace. This shift represented a significant change from the 1987 National Demonstration Project and highlighted that healthcare is no longer protected from the realities of the market.

The Patient Protection and Affordable Care Act (PPACA) of 2010 brought strong governmental forces to bear to drive innovation in healthcare as a way to reduce costs and improve quality. Provisions within the PPACA speak directly to the application of data-driven quality improvement. The PPACA required CMS to seek value in healthcare. CMS initiated programs to promote value rather than volume and to limit payments for hospital-acquired conditions. It went further in penalizing hospitals with high readmission and mortality rates for specific diagnoses. Finally, it publicly reported the actual costs for episodes of care at the hospital level based on claims paid by Medicare.

In addition to efforts to address specific issues of quality and costs in healthcare, the American Reinvestment and Recovery Act (ARRA) of 2009 focused a spotlight on electronic information systems. ARRA provided billions of dollars in incentive payments to hospitals and individual providers who implemented electronic health records that met the requirements. This initiative funded a significant increase in the implementation of electronic information technology in healthcare organizations and became a major force in the redesign of workflows in hospitals and physician offices. Of all the initiatives, this effort may offer the greatest potential for moving healthcare in a new direction. By strongly encouraging hospitals and physician offices to redesign their work flows to incorporate electronic information systems into clinical care, ARRA promotes the use of electronic information systems to bring patient information and clinical decision support to all the members of the healthcare team in real time. This is disruptive to current clinical care because so much of it is still based on paper medical records. Once healthcare information technology becomes part of the care process, it will enable clinical teams to communicate and share information while care is being delivered. It also expands the availability of data for analysis of clinical care processes and outcomes (ARRA 2009).

Understanding the origins of industrial quality concepts and techniques provides a basis for comprehending the effects they will have on healthcare. The exuberance of creating massive quantities of goods at low cost had to be tempered by the equally great waste of products from defects. Confronting this dilemma brought forth the innovations of the Shewhart's control charts, the Toyota Production System and Motorola's pursuit of Six Sigma performance. Deming, Juran and others promoted the ideas of continuous process and quality improvement as a leadership function. Despite the clear advantages of these approaches, American industry's focus on quantity as profitable blinded it to the ultimate costs of poor quality. It was not until the competition from Japan came ashore that American industry recognized the threat and the losses were already great.

American healthcare is reacting to the comparison with improvements in other industries and the demands of healthcare consumers and payers and in the same way that American industry initially responded to the emergence of the Toyota Production System and Six Sigma. While appearing to embrace industrial quality and using the language of continuous quality improvement, American healthcare in its essence continues to cling to the traditional definitions of quality based on the high utilization of hospital technology and physician specialization that evolved over 100 years.

Like American industry before it, American healthcare stands on the edge of a major change, and quality will be the instrument of transformation. This change will not arise from physicians or hospitals or from within healthcare. It will not come directly from the government or employers or insurers. It will come from the choices of individual healthcare consumers as they are asked to bear more of the direct costs of their own healthcare. The choices they make will shape the healthcare industry of the future.

Chapter 3

Quality-Driven Healthcare

3.1 Introduction

As American healthcare entered the 2000s, it brought over
100 years of traditions and cultural structures that exalted
the role of the physician and the hospital as the guardians of
healthcare and quality of life in America. It ran directly into
the radiation of cost controls, process standardization and
demands for predictable outcomes and zero defects that had
become hallmarks of industrial quality. Compared with healthcare in the world, American healthcare appeared to be a drain
on the lifeblood of the country. The cure, demanded by the
government and industry, was a massive infusion of industrial quality.

This chapter examines the effects of industrial quality on
American healthcare. Industrial quality is rooted in mass production in which the tolerance for waste and error progressed
to nearly zero. In this environment, the ability to compete
successfully in the marketplace is based on near-perfect delivery of exactly what the customer is willing to purchase. For
healthcare, historical developments have led to methods of

production and concepts of quality that are very different from industrial quality. The convergence of these two views results in dramatic changes in healthcare.

The next section, "Deconstructing 20th Century Healthcare," portrays images of 20th century healthcare as part of life in the local community and local hospital. This is referred to as a deconstruction of American healthcare because each person that reads it will bring memories of earlier times in which the person shared in these images and understanding about the way healthcare fits into life. These images also provide the canvas for observing the way the infusion of industrial quality into healthcare contrasts and conflicts with the older images. In these 20th century images of healthcare, the solid and stable world of the local community celebrates the mysteries and benefits of the local hospitals and physicians that serve the people.

Almost unnoticed from this perspective and more frightening, the images of healthcare on the national level arise like clouds on the horizon and cast shadows on the practices of healthcare in the towns across the country. The costs of healthcare and the quality concerns that are seemingly invisible locally at the end of the 20th century suddenly appear as threats to the local hospital and physicians. With this as background, Section 3.3, "Lean and Six Sigma and Industrialized Healthcare," uses the lens of Lean and Six Sigma to understand how the application of industrial quality clashes with the 20th century model and the reasons for the resistance to the changes it produces. This chapter identifies the transitions that healthcare is experiencing as it moves from the 20th century to the 21st century with the application of industrial quality.

3.2 Deconstructing 20th Century Healthcare

The historic development of American healthcare presented up to this point provides the context for recognizing the way in which technology and professionalization, information management and the financial processes evolved during the 20th century to create the uniquely American healthcare experience. This background serves as the basis for deconstructing 20th century healthcare by describing the way it exists today at the juncture of the past that created it and the industrialization that is changing it.

The deconstruction refers to the descriptions of the processes and practices of healthcare at the local community level that enable you to recognize the elements of 20th century healthcare that may resonate in your own experiences. As you consider these images and the culture and values they portray, the fundamental fabric of healthcare that is so resistant to change becomes clearer, as does the need for change to occur. It also provides a basis for understanding why industrialization is the instrument of change needed and why it is so difficult to apply to healthcare. Approaching this at the microsystem level provides a simpler picture for drawing meaningful insights into the whole. Healthcare, after all, is delivered at the local level one patient at a time.

Most of us can name the hospital where we were born. We remember the closest hospital in the communities where we grew up and the relatives who may have died there. We can recall trips to the Emergency Department after an accident. In setting the stage for understanding 20th century healthcare as it exists in communities across the country, it is appropriate to begin with this local hospital that we recall. In most American communities, the hospital is a highly visible landmark with an architectural structure unique to its function and prominent signage directing people to its location. Whether it is a contemporary or traditional structure, the hospital is clearly recognizable and plays a prominent place in the consciousness of the community.

Often people in the community can describe the history of the hospital and the pride that they feel about its success. In many cases, physicians in the area often provided the initial funding or even the home that served as the original structure for the hospital. Over the years, the local hospital structure and operation evolved and expanded as new technology and new services were added. Much of the pride associated with the local hospital is the way it serves as a symbol of the quality of life in the community and the ability of the community to provide its residents with the best healthcare. Whenever new technology or a new patient care unit is opened in the local hospital, it is prominently displayed in the newspaper with local dignitaries clustered around cutting ribbons. Newcomers to the community, businesses looking to open offices in the area and, of course, the recruitment of new physicians to the area always bring attention to the valuable role of the hospital in creating a higher standard of living for the community.

The board of the local hospital consists of prominent business, medical and community leaders. The board members view their participation in its governance as a symbol of their own status in the community. Reports on the successes and failures of the hospital appear in the local press following board meetings. Any changes in room rates and other charges and their influence on the hospital's bottom line are scrutinized with serious concern to ensure that there is no indication that the local hospital is not doing well. Debates about building plans or changes in services at the hospital often spill into the daily conversations of people in the community.

The hospital board members are often leading contributors to the hospital. Whenever new construction or purchases of new equipment are considered, these local benefactors are often visible in their support and contributions. In recognition of these gifts, names are added to rooms or to commemorative walls with plaques to recognize the contributors. Many business people also profit by serving on the local hospital board and learning of new developments and new physicians recruited to the community. The hospital board relies upon the medical staff at the hospital for guidance on types of services, the equipment to purchase, the facilities to provide and the quality of the care.

The local hospital serves as the coordinating center of healthcare activities in the community, particularly in smaller communities across the country. There may be other sources of healthcare in the community, such as the public health department, American Red Cross, and local pharmacies, but the hospital, with its meeting rooms, food services, management and healthcare professionals and financial resources, serves as the core of support for community activities that involve healthcare.

The centrality of the hospital in the consciousness and the lives of the people in communities across America today is testimony to the way that this particular institution forms the heart of healthcare. It has the latest technology and medical care and serves as the foundation for the healthcare delivery system in the community. It is an important asset to the community in recruiting businesses and medical professionals to the area. Finally, the hospital is a status symbol in differentiating the community from other smaller communities and attracts leading citizens to invest their time and resources in support of this important institution.

It is not hard to imagine a scene in which a physician is standing in front of the hospital and making a statement about the latest healthcare developments in the community. For many of us, the pediatrician or general practitioner of our childhood remains a symbol of help and hurt. In terms of the community, there is often a type of reverence for an elderly physician who served many years in the local hospital or delivered thousands of babies. In whatever setting, the physician stands out in the life of the community as the preeminent professional who takes care of us and guides our families through the tragedies, the joys and the end of life using the technology at the hospital. It is hard to overstate the strength of the paternalistic image of physicians within communities and the relationships that develop between physicians and their communities. Their personal relationships with families in the community are often recalled by people long after the physicians retire.

It is not difficult to understand the authority of a professional in the local hospital and in the local community. Beyond the personal relationships, physicians are often the most educated individuals in the community, with university and medical degrees and board certifications from professional associations within their particular specialties. Their practices are sources of revenue within the community and their patient admissions support the local hospital. Losing a physician from the community is a serious issue, particularly if only one or two of a particular specialty practice in the area because of the loss of the service and the way it might affect the local hospital.

Physicians are the source of employment for nurses and other staff retained by the hospital to meet their needs. They serve as pivotal figures in the delivery systems in terms of attracting patients, prescribing medications and other supplies that are dispensed by local pharmacies and other suppliers and, of course, sending patients to the hospital. The hospital serves as a resource enabling the physicians to practice in the local community rather than remaining in the larger cities where they are usually trained.

Within the local hospital, the physicians belong to the medical staff that has its own organization separate from the bureaucratic organization of the hospital. The medical staff conducts its business through the medical executive committee and through the meetings of the groups of specialists who work at the hospital and various committees of the medical staff that report to the medical executive committee. It is ostensibly under the direction of the hospital board, but the board is not trained to make clinical decisions and often does not have the education or training to understand the inner workings of the patient care processes or the medical staff.

Applications for medical staff membership are processed by hospital staff, but the application requires approval of the medical staff and the board. The board depends heavily on the medical staff to evaluate the licensure, education, and demonstrated clinical competence of applicants for medical staff membership.

Physicians admitting patients to the hospital design many of the processes of care to meet their own needs with the support of the hospital. The nursing staff learns the preferences of physicians and adapts its care processes to reflect these preferences. The physicians admit and care for patients in the hospital based on schedules adapted to their office schedules. They admit patients on certain days and perform procedures on certain days and conduct rounds at particular times. Physicians document the care of their patients in handwritten progress notes and order tests or medications with handwritten orders. These notes and orders are required to meet the criteria established by the medical staff rules and regulations, but there is considerable latitude granted to the physicians in their documentation. The quality of the care delivered to the patients is ultimately determined by the physicians who are viewed as the experts and sources of knowledge about how care is to be delivered.

Physician relationships within the hospital and the community form an integral part of the process for delivering healthcare. Patients depend upon physicians for referrals to specialists. As physicians seek to build their practices, they develop reputations among their colleagues for taking good care of patients and, in response, they receive referrals. Physicians perceived as providing poor care by other physicians or not responding well to their colleagues are recognized over time and may be encouraged to leave by not receiving referrals. This informal system of recognizing the quality of care and the status of professional relationships is an integral part of the professional affiliation of the medical community. Relationships with other physicians are a key part of successful practices and an important way in which physicians try to maintain the quality of care in the local community.

Each day, physicians practice as they have been trained and, as members of the medical staff, they may be called upon to evaluate the quality of care provided by their colleagues. In most cases, physicians in leadership positions talk with colleagues who seem to be having problems and discuss the problems on a personal level. However, if the problems continue or are severe enough, then there is a formal process for review of the care delivered by a physician. Membership in the medical staff is organized as a professional affiliation structured according to the regulatory standards from Medicare and accrediting agencies. These agencies require the local medical staff to have an organizational structure and bylaws and evaluate the care provided by its membership. This review is built into the regular reappointment to the medical staff in which the leadership reviews the records of the local physicians in order to determine whether they should be reappointed to the medical staff. Review by colleagues of the work of particular physicians is also conducted when bad outcomes of care become known to the hospital or other members of the medical staff or through complaints from patients.

When a quality issue is identified in the care of a patient, a review of one physician by another, described as "peer review," is done. The review is often assigned to a physician who holds a leadership position in the medical staff. The reviewing physician is ideally in the same specialty with at least comparable expertise. The review involves the care of a particular patient in most cases and the results are the professional opinion of the reviewer on whether the standard of care in the opinion of the reviewing physician was provided to the patient. The standard of care sounds like a solid understanding of the way care should be provided, but in reality the standard of care for 20th century physicians was the standard accepted by the local hospital medical staff. The overall quality of care, however, is based on the consensus of the local hospital and local medical staff.

In addition to overseeing the quality of care delivered in the hospital, the relationship between the physicians and their patients makes the physician an advocate for patients with complaints concerning hospital care. Physicians are often the voice of patients back to the hospital administration. As they admit patients to the hospital and follow up with them after discharge, the patients often relay to the physician what is good or bad about their hospital experience. This information relayed to the hospital becomes part of the overall assessment of the quality of hospital care as perceived by the patients. Changes at the local hospital level often result from conversations between physicians and hospital leadership on the opinions of patients about care and conditions at the hospital.

The picture of hospitals and physicians described here incorporates the basic values and structures of healthcare as it evolved in the 20th century and as it exists today. In communities across the country, healthcare is individual physicians and local hospitals operating under local controls in which informal relationships between professionals and trust between physicians and patients structure the system of care. It is not difficult to see the insular nature of local healthcare and the way in which the delivery of healthcare is shaped by the culture and values of the community.

Hidden within this local healthcare community are the assumptions that developed during the 20th century on the nature of healthcare and the way it should be delivered. These assumptions form the basis for decisions pertaining to the delivery of healthcare and the evaluation of quality. The concepts hidden within American healthcare at the local level are that (1) the hospital is the source of healthcare, (2) individual physicians determine the care of patients and (3) the quality of healthcare is based on the technology and physician specialists and is evaluated by physician peer review. New developments in healthcare are viewed from the perspective of culture and values and beliefs of the local healthcare community.

The problems in healthcare that motivate Washington or state capitals to propose changes may seem far removed from the reality of the local network of hospitals and physicians that measure their success in the confidence and support of the communities they serve. They have techniques for absorbing new regulations and practices through incremental changes at the local level. These changes, for the most part, are not the radical changes advocated in the national forums, but rather minor changes designed to create compliance with minimal disruption. It is not surprising that the attempts at the national level to raise the question of the cost of care and the level of quality fail to resonate at the local level. Physician reactions to the National Demonstration Project in the late 1980s involved pointing to the fundamental disconnect between the production of automobiles and the care of people. For many, the concept of industrializing healthcare and referring to patients as customers does not resonate with their own experiences.

American healthcare at the local level resists the use of industrial quality methods as a means for improvement, because they are inconsistent with the culture and practice of healthcare in the communities. Hospitals and their medical staffs assess quality on a personal level as they evaluate the outcomes of individual patients. They do not see the need for statistical process control to determine whether a patient received good care. Each patient is viewed as unique and requiring a plan of care that the physician develops for this specific patient. To standardize care in the same way that you standardize industrial production processes is viewed as unacceptable and foreign to the training and experiences of professionals.

It is clear that industrial quality is very different from the assumptions that shaped healthcare in the past. Healthcare has been through many changes in the past 100 years, but nothing comparable to forcing a different production and quality model on healthcare has been attempted. Such ideas are viewed as radical and misinformed from the perspective of the

20th century and disruptive to the way care should be delivered. It is frequently interpreted as betrayal of the values of American healthcare.

What provides the incentive to follow such an unusual path? The forces for change are summarized in the Institute of Medicine's (IOM's) report *Best Care at Lower Cost,* which compared American healthcare to other industries and questioned why it should be considered differently. With waste estimated at $750 billion a year, healthcare compares unfavorably in the report with shopping, banking, home building and airlines. This made a strong statement that the environment within which healthcare functions has changed and it is time for healthcare to accept 21st century industrial quality and production concepts that have worked so well in other industries as the means for the transformation.

Unlike other industries, however, healthcare retains its fundamental craftsman nature within the microstructure of patients, physicians, traditions and culture of the local hospitals and local communities. Community values and laws pertaining to healthcare and even the financial structures of the past continue today. American healthcare requires the application of Lean and Six Sigma industrialization at the hospital level and practitioner level to initiate the transition from the established 20th century model to a new 21st century vision of healthcare that fits the needs of the communities of the future.

3.3 Lean and Six Sigma and Industrialized Healthcare

At the end of the 20th century, the financial concessions that led to the passage of the original Medicare legislation created a system of care for the elderly but also created a significant drain on the federal budget that exceeded expectations. With cost-based reimbursement of care and other generous provisions designed to promote acceptance of the program, Medicare expenses rose higher and faster than had been anticipated. In less than 10 years, it was clear that changes were needed to restrain the rate of increases in the costs of Medicare (Stevens 1999).

Medicare did something else that would have a profound effect on American healthcare. As part of the federal government paying Medicare claims, all of those claims ended up in a central database repository. For the first time in American healthcare history, information on costs and codes for specific care from massive numbers of individual patients were centralized and accessible through the Medicare database. Mining this amazing data repository using the growing power of computers provided researchers with a detailed picture of the way American healthcare actually worked. One of the best examples of this was the Dartmouth Atlas of Healthcare (2014):

> For more than 20 years, the Dartmouth Atlas Project has documented glaring variations in how medical resources are distributed and used in the United States. The project uses Medicare data to provide information and analysis about national, regional, and local markets, as well as hospitals and their affiliated physicians.

Studies of the Medicare data indicated that the costs and variation in care in American healthcare at the local level did not result from variations in the health of patients. It was variation in local markets as a result of physicians who made care decisions for reasons that were not based on best practice. The protests that the high cost of American healthcare made it the best healthcare in the world faded in light of comparisons with quality and mortality rates in other countries and the variation demonstrated by the Medicare data. The costs borne by Americans did not prolong life or quality of life in any meaningful way; it simply cost more.

The IOM reports indicated that efforts from within health-care to improve quality, safety and cost problems failed and that healthcare policymakers turned to unorthodox methods for addressing these issues. In the search for a way to address these concerns, the changes that had occurred in the industrial sector of the American economy appeared to offer potential answers. Reminiscent of the experience of American industry that viewed itself as the premier manufacturing engine in the world until Toyota took over that role, American health-care woke up to the data from around the world and its own practices to recognize the fallacy of its assumptions (IOM 2012, 2013).

The success of Toyota in the marketplace was the most obvious signal that the company had the ability to build good cars, but the real mystery—and the most frightening to American industry—was the ability of Toyota to build good cars while achieving a profit margin on each car that was significantly greater than that experienced in the United States. The ability of Toyota to produce high-quality cars for much less cost caught the attention of government and payers look-ing to improve American healthcare. This was the part that was most applicable to the issues affecting healthcare. Many theories were proposed by American industry to suggest that the Japanese were doing nothing different, but had advan-tages other than their methods of manufacturing. They had lower healthcare costs, government subsidies, Japanese culture and other advantages denied to American manufacturing. As Toyota freely shared its methods, however, it became evident that the company had found a better way to produce high-quality cars for less and this made Toyota a company of inter-est to innovative thinkers in American healthcare (Womack, Jones and Roos 2007).

During the same period, a new way to improve qual-ity emerged in an American company that needed to reduce defects. Drawing on the concepts associated with W. Edwards Deming, Joseph Juran and others, Motorola's quality team put together a program using the best of the concepts on process improvement and the quality tools to operationalize the ideas for performance improvement. The Motorola program focused in a unique way on the goal of reducing defects and defective products to the very low rate of 3.4 defects per million opportunities or a statistical level of six sigma. It applied improvement tools and statistical process control techniques throughout the company to achieve this goal and was the first company to win the federal government's Malcolm Baldrige National Quality Award. This system offered hope for American healthcare, which had been severely chastised by the IOM for its errors in 1999 (Harry and Schroeder 2006).

Of all the improvement programs used by American industry, the Toyota Production System (or Lean) and Six Sigma, as it was eventually defined by GE and others best exemplifies the concepts and techniques for improving quality and reducing costs that changed American industry. As 20th century American healthcare's cost, quality and safety issues became more apparent and as new ways of improving processes and reducing errors produced excellent results in industry, healthcare could no longer maintain its claims of uniqueness and acceptable performance.

The implicit challenge to the traditions and practices of healthcare in America that developed in the 20th century arise from the unfavorable comparison of healthcare to industry. American healthcare can no longer protest its uniqueness as a basis for operating at a level of cost and quality inconsistent with other industries in America as described by the IOM 2012 report. To fit within the new environment created by American industry, healthcare must commit to using industrialized production methods and quality improvement concepts and techniques because no other approach offers the means for achieving the changes required to address the quality and cost concerns.

When the industrial quality concepts and techniques of Lean and Six Sigma are applied fully to healthcare organizations, there is a clash of cultures and a resulting transformative effect that forces healthcare organizations to transition to a 21st century model of healthcare. The application of industrial production and quality brings to light the concepts and values inherent in the 20th century model of healthcare that are so familiar as to be invisible. Once these are exposed through industrialization, the contrasts between the past and the future in healthcare organizations become clearer and organizations are challenged to change. This is the foundational work that must occur to prepare healthcare organizations for the additional changes that are required by the industrial and healthcare environments of the 21st century. If industrialization is not fully applied to transform the production and quality methods of healthcare organizations, the challenge to the existing values and practices is muted. This creates a confusing mixture of cultures that prevents the leadership and staff from clearly seeing the changes required to transition to a 21st century healthcare organization.

The reason that organizations may not fully implement industrial quality is that healthcare, like industry, finds it difficult to let go of its successful past and to embrace a new and untried future. The way healthcare is delivered in most hospitals across the country reflects the long-held values and traditions of 20th century healthcare that continue to operate successfully in healthcare organizations in local communities across the country. In order for these to change and for organizations to proceed on the path to 21st century healthcare, the full force of Lean and Six Sigma must be released in the organization to challenge and transform these underlying values, structures and practices. Organizations must commit to these methods and practice them consistently to begin this transition.

As healthcare organizations recognize the need for change and begin to apply industrial concepts and techniques from Lean and Six Sigma, the initial reaction within the organization is to challenge the new methods as unacceptable to healthcare. The resistance comes as industrialization requires new terms and definitions in healthcare for the essential elements of industrial production. Healthcare is required to define the customer, product, value and the flow of processes as the first steps in implementing the industrialization.

The first challenge that arises with industrialization in healthcare is the identification of the customer. Lean and Six Sigma begin with the customer defined as the purchaser of the product, because the customer's needs or expectations and willingness to pay define the product. The goal in industry is to create a product or service that the customer is willing to purchase. The application of Lean focuses on producing that product as efficiently as possible by decreasing the time from the order to the finished product and reducing all forms of waste to their lowest possible levels. The goal for Six Sigma is to produce the product to the exact specifications of the customer without defects to ensure the satisfaction of the patient as well as to reduce the costs associated with defects. In both systems it is the customer, defined as the one who pays for the product, who defines the product that is to be produced (Ohno 1988).

The importance of identifying the customer seems straightforward in most industries. The difficulty for American healthcare in identifying the customer is one of the key indicators that healthcare as it exists today operates differently from industry and points to the reason that industrialization will require a major shift in the fundamentals of healthcare. It is also an indicator of the transformative nature of Lean and Six Sigma when applied to healthcare.

Defining the customer is not something that is actually a part of American healthcare's tradition. Healthcare did not have customers in the 20th century. Healthcare had patients. The word "patient" arises from Latin and Greek roots for "suffer" or "suffering." As used in healthcare, it relates to the status of the patient as suffering, but it does not denote the role of the patient as the customer. Throughout the latter part of the 20th century, there really is no individual who can be identified as the customer in healthcare that approximates the understanding of the customer in industry. Identifying who in healthcare is the customer based on the definition of paying for the product or service is an essential first step in Lean and Six Sigma.

Applying to healthcare the concept of the customer as the one who pays for the product creates confusion and often provokes an angry reaction from clinical staff that healthcare does not have customers. This reaction is actually true from the clinical service perspective, because the payment process in healthcare that developed in the 20th century and the professionalization of the physician obscure the identity of the person actually purchasing the service and make it difficult for the customer role to be clearly identified.

Historically, patients paid the physician working as a craftsman in private practice. The patient and the customer were the same. Early in the 20th century, hospital prepayment appeared but the patient could still be identified with the payment and the services purchased because the patient was buying days in the hospital. Again, the patient and the customer were the same. In the middle of the century, the process switched to insurance and the payer switched to the employer and the government. Employers paid directly or took a portion of employee pay and applied it to health insurance. The government used taxes to obtain the funds for Medicare. The employers and the government took on responsibility for paying for the insurance that paid for the care received by the patient.

Healthcare insurance paid the hospital and the physician for their services on behalf of the patient. This payment process removed the patient completely from the actual role of purchasing healthcare services. The billing and payments were handled between the insurer and the providers of care. In the payment processes for healthcare at the end of the 20th century, the patient is the recipient of the services as a patient but is not recognized as the customer. The insurer is the payer using the premiums from the employers and taxes from the government, but neither the insurer nor the employers or government actually receives the services.

If healthcare has no customer that specifically purchases the product and uses the product, then who are the people whom healthcare should consider as potential customers? The physician is actually treated in 20th century healthcare as the de facto customer due to the professionalization that gives the physician sole power to order services. The identification of the physician as the customer of hospitals and healthcare services created the basis for many of healthcare's quality and cost issues. The physician does not pay for the services, so the costs of the services are of no concern for the physician. If the physician is the customer but bears no responsibility for costs, then anything that the physician believes will be helpful in testing and procedures from a strictly clinical perspective becomes the product and cost is not a concern of this customer. The physician as customer, therefore, creates a production process that promotes high utilization of services without regard for costs. This is the production problem facing healthcare.

The physician as the customer defines the criteria for the services that the healthcare organization creates. Since time is a key quality characteristic for physicians, convenience and speed and ease of access for physicians are important to hospitals in meeting the needs of this customer. Waiting rooms make perfect sense with the physician as the customer, because the physician defines quality by having patients available when the physician is ready to see the patients. It is not surprising that hospitals should be full of waiting rooms for patients in which the patient's time is not a concern but the physician's convenience is a key quality issue. Identifying the physician as the customer of healthcare creates the issues that healthcare is trying to improve and is, therefore, not useful in the industrialization process.

The patient as the recipient of the services is the most logical person to serve as the customer, but the patient is not usually involved in the payment process nor is the patient the one who orders the service or product or identifies the characteristics that make it worth purchasing. Because of the lack of a direct connection between the patient and the purchase of the services, the ability of the patient to serve as the customer is compromised. Only a customer that is paying for a product finds it meaningful to spend time in defining the product and evaluating the product once it is delivered. Healthcare, like any industry, seeks out the payer and responds to payers' requirements in producing the services. The patient, however, does not fall into this category. Even the designation of "patient" tends to obscure any role as a potential customer.

The purpose of industrialization in healthcare is to address the cost and quality issues, and identifying the customer is the first step in that process. Based on the 20th century model, healthcare has no clearly identified customer based on industry requirements. To fully implement industrialization, healthcare needs to identify a customer that functions as a customer. Due to changes in healthcare payment processes and the move to high-deductible insurance plans and higher total out-of-pocket requirements, patients in the future will bear more responsibility for payment of services and will, therefore, reenter the marketplace as direct purchasers of healthcare services. This change in the environment offers support for the patient to serve as the customer for applying Lean and Six Sigma methods to improve healthcare.

If the physician is no longer considered the customer, then the status of the patient as the customer represents a significant challenge to healthcare What does it mean to healthcare if the patient is the customer for the purposes of Lean and Six Sigma? As healthcare organizations implement Lean and Six Sigma with the patient as the customer, they will find it useful to recognize the people they serve as having dual status of patient and customer in the production and improvement processes. There are times in the processes of care where it is the patient role that needs to be recognized. There are other times when the customer role needs to be the focus. By using the metaphor of a patient-customer for the people they serve, healthcare organizations can transition to a better understanding of the way to respond to people in their various roles. The patient-customers are patients as they comply with physician orders and are treated by healthcare professionals. They are customers in their role of identifying the types of products and the quality of services they want to purchase and the value that makes them willing to pay for them.

In recognizing patient-customers, healthcare organizations will need to develop ways to determine what these new customers expect in the services they receive and what they are willing to pay to receive them. Physicians viewed as customers had easy access to healthcare resources because they also functioned as leaders in the production process. It will take the full implementation of Lean and Six Sigma to create the organizational imperative for focusing on patient-customers in the future. Lean and Six Sigma require healthcare organizations to reevaluate their traditional views of physicians and insurers as their customers, to recognize the patient-customer and to develop new processes and methods to respond to this new status.

Identifying the customer is the first step, because this provides the basis for identifying the product or service and the criteria the customer requires to be met before paying. Addressing the question of the product represents the second step as healthcare seeks to use industrialization for improvement. As with the identification of the customer, product identification creates confusion in healthcare organizations. This confusion arises from the difference between the historical goals of healthcare in the 20th century and the modern goals of products in Lean and Six Sigma methods. If the industrial criteria for a product or service are that the production process makes material changes in the product and the customer is willing to purchase it, then the patients meet the criteria of a product in their role as a patient. Healthcare changes the state of the patient and this makes it very different from other services. In applying Lean and Six Sigma industrial quality concepts to 20th century American healthcare, the patient can be defined as the product of healthcare. That seems counterintuitive since people are not often viewed as Lean and Six Sigma products in healthcare (Ohno 1988).

The product status of the patient has been assumed by healthcare throughout the 20th century in practice, even though it was hidden beneath the paternalism of physicians and nurses who controlled all aspects of the patient's care during hospitalization. In the end, the compliance of the patient, like the malleability of the materials for industrial production, was the expectation of the healthcare system and the understood role of the patient. The patient was not treated as a customer or involved in the design or production of his or her healthcare process for most of the 20th century. The patient was the product that was improved and either was or was not defective at the end of the hospital stay in Lean and Six Sigma terms.

In order for healthcare organizations to overcome the past and prepare for the future, it is time to recognize the dual status of the patient as the product of healthcare from the clinical perspective and the patient as the customer from the perspective of designing and improving healthcare services. The designation of patient-customer provides a useful metaphor for incorporating these roles into the implementation of Lean and Six Sigma.

With the patient-customer identified, the discovery of the new definition of value within healthcare is the next challenge. The full implementation of Lean and Six Sigma requires that healthcare organizations redefine value. When the patient-customer is included in the determination of value, the processes of care change significantly and there is a dramatic shift in the way the entire healthcare organization views its processes. For example, when the patient-customer defines value as easy access to services without waiting, the patient-customer's time suddenly becomes a measure of the quality of the services. Waiting is viewed as a defect and not valuable to the patient-customer. As services are designed, patients as customers express their preferences about the services and what they are willing to pay to receive better or faster services. It is at this point that the preferences of patient-customers become important in the design and operation of processes in healthcare organizations. Participation by patient-customers in the development of services becomes a high priority to ensure that the expectations of patient-customers are clearly understood and that steps in processes add value that they are willing to purchase (Ohno 1988).

Identifying what is valuable to patient-customers is critically important in helping healthcare organizations to identify what is waste and needs to be eliminated. If patients are not willing to pay for a service, then organizations need to seriously consider either eliminating it or redesigning it to make it valuable to patients. Eliminating waste involves identifying the steps that add value and identifying non-value-added steps that represent waste. By eliminating steps that do not add value to the product, the organization helps to reduce costs and increase patient-customer satisfaction and ultimately lower the prices for services. They are more likely to choose quality services that cost less, just as consumers chose Toyota vehicles over Detroit's cars. The implementation of industrial quality focuses attention on the quality of the services and the elimination of any defects in the services from the patient-customer perspective. These defects may directly affect the patient or may be waste within hospital processes that do not add value. This places an emphasis on the culture of the organization as accepting the importance of eliminating waste and defects and continuously improving services to meet the expectations of patients (Ohno 1988).

Finally, the flow of healthcare processes is a powerful aspect of Lean that is problematic to healthcare but offers healthcare organizations the opportunity to make significant improvements. Flow describes the movement of products or services through the processes that leads to the final outcomes. Flow is most easily understood when applied to support services in hospitals such as laundry, dietary and environmental services. From a Lean perspective, the flow of the process to clean a room or supply laundry begins when the need for a clean room or more towels is recognized and the department that provides the services is notified of the need. Flow in this type of process is easy to see as the delivery of the materials or the arrival of staff to clean the room occurs. If there is a delay, it is easy to see the delay as breakdown in the flow.

When the flow of patient care is considered, the ability to see the flow is reduced because there may be no physical movement by the patient. Like diners in a restaurant who spend their entire meal at one table, patients in the hospital may spend their entire stay in the hospital in one bed. The flow in these instances is the flow of the process that moves the diners to the completion of their meal and the patients to their discharge from the hospital. Identifying delays in these types of process flows is important because they represent important customer satisfiers and important opportunities to reduce costs. Lean and Six Sigma point to the process flows around the patient and identify that these flows combine to create the flow of the patient's movement toward discharge. Responding to this aspect of the improvement in the production of healthcare is a challenge to traditional 20th century healthcare because it requires intensive flowcharting and measurement to clearly identify the flows and to identify the bottlenecks and delays that cause the patient's care process and movement toward discharge to break down. When these support systems process flows have been maximized, then the movement of patients through the overall flow is improved (Ohno 1988).

Flow as a part of Lean quality pushes healthcare organizations to recognize the interconnected nature of processes and the need for standardization in these processes to ensure quality. In responding to this aspect of industrialization, healthcare organizations often encounter the dilemma of trying to improve processes that involve physicians or other professionals. In healthcare organizations throughout the 20th century, physicians played a dominant role in the design of processes. From the admission of patients to documentation in the medical record to scheduling procedures, most hospital services were designed with the physician, rather than the patient, in mind. In many cases, these process designs were based on the convenience to the physician even if it meant delays for the patients. In addition to the focus on the needs of physicians by the hospital, healthcare professionals often change processes for a variety of reasons. This customization of the processes may lead to variations in quality and inconsistent outcomes. It is within these contexts that industrialization promotes the organizational recognition of the definitive role of the patient-customer for identifying value in processes. The full implementation of Lean and Six Sigma that includes the support of leadership works to overcome individual preferences to improve the flow of processes and move healthcare organizations forward in their transition to 21st century healthcare.

As healthcare organizations work to understand and redesign processes based on new definitions of patient-customer, product, value and flow, Lean and Six Sigma offer an organization a method to follow as a structure for improvement. A common improvement process used in connection with Lean and Six Sigma is "define–measure–analyze–improve–control" (DMAIC). This framework for Six Sigma is also often used to structure Lean initiatives and provides an improvement methodology for establishing a culture of continuous improvement in the pursuit of perfection wherever work is performed.

Continuous improvement is a necessary part of industrialization in healthcare, because the expectations of patient-
customers continuously change as products and services
reach new levels of quality at lower costs. The application of
improvement methods such as DMAIC challenges healthcare
organizations to identify customers, services and values.

Walking through the steps in DMAIC as they may be
applied to healthcare organizations provides an introduction
to the types of issues that may create confusion or will need
to be addressed to support industrialization. This review of
common questions that arise with the application of DMAIC to
healthcare improvement efforts is not designed to be compre-
hensive or to reflect the experiences of all healthcare organizations. It reflects common issues that come up in the attempts
to implement Lean and Six Sigma to provide examples of
how the inherent structures and values of healthcare organizations based on their 20th century heritage create conflict
with industrialization.

The first step in DMAIC, "define," refers to creating a clear
statement of the rationale for improving a particular process
and identifying the key participants, such as the champion,
company team, suppliers and customers that will be involved.
Even in this early stage, healthcare organizations struggle
to develop a clear understanding of the process that needs
improvement because care processes are defined by individual professionals and the suppliers and customers within the
process are hard to identify. This step also includes the business reason for undertaking the improvement. Costs associated
with patient care are notoriously difficult to identify within
care processes due to the lack of clear process steps and
healthcare's problems with activity costs. Healthcare often falls
back on the chargemaster to estimate costs, but the charges
are often widely exaggerated to accommodate special insurance provisions. The problems identified in the completion of
the define phase need to be resolved organizationally in order
for improvements to occur.

Once the team has completed the define phase, the next step is "measurement." In measurement, industrial quality requires the ability to collect data that specifically relate to the processes in order to establish a baseline for the current performance and to identify any opportunities to improve. Measurement presents healthcare with two problems that are not easily resolved. The first problem is the ability to collect data on processes. Most healthcare organizations lack electronic data collection capability. Electronic data collection on the industrial scale was not available even in the most sophisticated healthcare organizations until very recently. Data from care processes require painfully slow manual abstraction by clinical staff. Typically, the sample sizes are small and in most cases the methodology is extremely primitive in comparison with industry. The results are marginally accurate at best and reveal little but the most obvious process issues. As integrated information systems become a part of healthcare organizations and the importance of data to the quality of the care is recognized, healthcare organizations will implement systems that make data available at the point of care to monitor the quality of care as it is delivered. This will lead healthcare workers to actively recognize variation in the processes of care and involve management in improving processes quickly.

The second problem is the lack of standardized processes, particularly in the clinical areas. Most clinical processes are not specifically defined except for key activities that may be addressed by policies and procedures. These key activities may have required steps such as sterile techniques and assessments, but the processes within which they function are rarely defined. For physicians, the policies and procedures and even online order sets are often viewed as guidelines that are not necessarily required. Due to the lack of standardization, data to even define the process can be difficult to obtain and may not represent the actual processes. To help with these issues, a flowchart or value stream map or spaghetti diagram of movement within a process provides data in the form of a graphical image that describes the processes and identifies areas with delays or waste or lack of standardization. This image of the processes presents the current state and is followed by an image of the future state that identifies potential opportunities for improvement and how they would change the process.

Once data have been obtained, the "analyze" phase uses the data collected to identify ways to improve the process. The results of the data collection are reviewed to assess the actual state of the process and to identify improvements. Most healthcare organizations find the process data analysis frustrating because of the lack of training in statistical process control and other forms of data analysis and the lack of support staff able to assist with the work. Whereas frontline staff in industry uses data to monitor ongoing daily operations, healthcare rarely has the capability and staff is rarely able to access either system information or clinical information beyond the individual patient to actually see the data related to processes. Part of the full implementation of Lean and Six Sigma is to drive data accessibility and analysis to the frontlines of care to enable the employees to access and interpret real-time data concerning care processes and to respond to the data with incremental improvements.

"Improvement" is the next phase and this is the heart of DMAIC. Process improvement has been a part of healthcare for several decades, but it has remained a project-based undertaking designed to address very specific problems. It is not a continuous, incremental process in which the work is improved on an ongoing basis through small changes. Actually attempting to improve processes is problematic in healthcare for two reasons. Most processes cross organizational departmental lines and require support from multiple management figures. Support for change is difficult to obtain and often the attempts to improve processes end in failure due to active resistance or a lack of support. The second difficulty that confronts efforts to improve processes in healthcare involves physicians and other professional staff. Improvements that require support or include changes in clinical processes often encounter significant resistance from clinical staff. In many cases, this resistance is a result of the effect of the change on a particular clinician's work processes. It may also involve clinical practice changes that are new and may not have the support from the clinical staff. For improvements to succeed, full implementation of industrialization is needed to build the support that is required. All areas of the organization must recognize the need for continuous improvement, the importance of supporting such initiatives and the commitment of the organization's leadership.

"Control" is required to standardize the improvement and to sustain the change, and this is the final stage of DMAIC. Once processes are improved to reflect best practices, controlling the processes to sustain the changes is accomplished through standardization. Standardization is not a strong point for healthcare because of turnover of staff, lack of time and resources for training staff on new processes, lack of consistent acceptance and support by leadership in all areas and the ability of clinical staff to use professional judgment to deviate from the new design of the processes. In 20th century healthcare, minimally defined processes built on the traditions of the organization and the preferences of the professional staff, rather than the patient, undermined attempts at standardization. For professionals, there is no sense of actual variation in the process. There are only individual patients and the tasks associated with the care of those patients. Continuous improvement efforts require standardization and this challenges the professional judgment of the physicians, nurses and therapists in shaping the care processes. The goal of achieving customer-defined products with a Six Sigma level of perfection is seldom even attempted because the level of variation is too great and the lack of consensus about the process does not support the required standardization. As healthcare organizations recognize the need for industrialization to create the platform for building 21st century healthcare organizations, the

importance of standardization to achieve high-quality outcomes and reduced costs becomes clearer.

DMAIC in conjunction with a variety of improvement tools
provides the foundation to support continuous improvement
within healthcare organizations. Industrialization empowers
healthcare organizations to see the pursuit of perfection as an
important aspect of the move toward 21st century healthcare
since perfection has not been a value that has been emphasized in healthcare. Perfection in healthcare carries an omi-
nous element because of the unpredictability of patients and
the complexity of patient care that may need to change as the
conditions of patients change. There is also a sense in which
perfection as it relates to the outcomes of patients creates
expectations that healthcare professionals find difficult to rec-
oncile with the many potentialities in patient care. Helping to
define the pursuit of perfection in the delivery of high-quality
care is an important aspect of the implementation of industrial
quality since it is the expectation of patients that healthcare
providers are always working to achieve perfect care.

In summary, the implementation of industrialized quality
as exemplified by Lean and Six Sigma brings into healthcare a
new set of values, concepts and techniques that were not part
of the American healthcare of the 20th century, but represent
important aspects of 21st century healthcare. Born out of limited resources in Japan and out of the need for defect-free production in America, Lean and Six Sigma and similar methods
of industrialization offer American healthcare the methods for
improvement and the redesign of healthcare that answers the
seemingly insoluble problems of healthcare costs and quality.

In gaining the benefits of industrialization, healthcare
must redefine the understanding of customer, product, value
and flow. American healthcare faces a future of diminishing
resources where waste of any kind will be a serious problem.
Producing exactly what patient-customers need and are willing to purchase replaces the tradition of doing everything that
can be done to see if anything helps. The new philosophy

of care means protecting patients from the potential harms associated with the excessive services by building processes that specifically address the expectations of patient-customers. The patient-customer challenges the 20th century model of professionally defined processes and requires healthcare to listen and learn and to structure the processes of healthcare to deliver care efficiently and consistently.

As healthcare embraces industrialization, the need to create the tools and infrastructure for continuous improvement and the pursuit of perfection become high priorities. Training staff in the concepts and techniques of Lean and Six Sigma to promote full industrialization offers a significant return on investment as the efforts to improve processes move from the meeting rooms to the day-to-day work of individuals. The use of electronic information systems that connect individuals and groups and provide information in real time about breakdowns in process flow supports more rapid responses to quality issues and improved production to meet Six Sigma levels of quality.

Healthcare in the 21st century will emerge out of the industrialization produced by Lean and Six Sigma and the expansion of sophisticated electronic information systems with increased efficiency and responsiveness to patient-customers. The more these initiatives are incorporated into healthcare organizations, the more these organizations begin to identify the essential areas that must change to adapt to the requirements of the 21st century model of care. The professionalization, bureaucratic fragmentation and archaic payment processes of 20th century healthcare crumble as industrialization pushes for results that satisfy the patient-customers.

Even as industrialization gains momentum, it is clear that industrialized healthcare is not the final stage. As the 20th century model is challenged by the values of industrialized quality and redesigned and restructured, the resulting healthcare delivery system operates at a different level of cost and quality.

Industrialization is the instrument of change, but it is not the goal of change. The goal of change is to discover a new type of healthcare. Passing through the industrialization phase sets the stage for the transitions that will lead to 21st century healthcare.

Chapter 4

Industrialized Healthcare and Organizational Transitions

4.1 Introduction

As healthcare organizations implement industrialization, 20th century values, structures and practices that are embedded in the organizations are highlighted. The redefinition of value by patient-customers rather than by the professionals, the creation of structures to support standardization and clinical process improvement and the adoption of processes that promote efficiency and eliminate waste and errors challenge the status quo. These aspects of the organization that contrast with the industrialized systems and values are forced to change to adapt to the environment within the organization.

These changes create the industrialization phase that moves the organizations from the 20th century model of healthcare to the 21st century model by promoting the values of mass production, the focus on cost, waste and customers inherent in industrial quality and the use of data to spur improvement. Areas of healthcare organizations that must be redesigned to

meet the needs of the future are identified through their conflict with industrialization. Like sparks flying as the grindstone
sharpens the blade, industrialization illuminates the dimensions of healthcare organization that reflect the 20th century.

As the industrialization process progresses, the dimensions
of organizations that are rooted in the 20th century become
clear and transition to a future state. This future state becomes
clearer as industrialization progresses toward full implementation, and the image of the 21st century healthcare organization
that appears serves to guide the progress of organizations
beyond the industrialization phase to the future. In 21st century healthcare, patient-customer defined values and needs
shape healthcare organizations in new ways. As complex
adaptive systems, 21st century healthcare organizations continuously evolve to absorb new technologies and care processes
and to link patients with the professional and technical support systems they need to manage their health.

If healthcare organizations are in a transitional phase in
which industrial quality challenges and changes the 20th century model of healthcare into the emergent 21st century
healthcare, then healthcare organizations should be able to
assess the progress they are making in moving from one
model to the next. Mapping this transition and the dynamics at
work provides an opportunity for healthcare leaders and their
organizations to understand what is happening and to accelerate their rate of transition into the 21st century so that they are
prepared to succeed in this new environment.

There are ten transitions that are critically important for
healthcare organizations to navigate in the progression to the
21st century model. These transitions begin as the 20th century roots of American healthcare organizations appear
through industrialization and transition to the 21st century as
the organizations change and evolve. Prior to industrialization, they were not evident because there was no conflict that
identified the need to transition these areas. There was simply

the continuation of the 20th century model. As industrialization moves through American healthcare organizations, the ten transitions appear and they define the shift that healthcare organizations must make if they are to adapt and succeed in a future that is very different from the past. These ten transitions are:

- Organizational structure
- Organizational relationships
- Leadership
- Innovation
- Production
- Delivery systems
- Information systems
- Finance
- Professionalism
- Metaphor

Each of these transitions consists of a continuum. One end of the continuum is the 20th century model of healthcare. The other end of the continuum is the 21st century model of healthcare. Organizations progress along the continuum as they move away from the 20th century model toward the 21st century in each of the transitions. The transitions appear as the application of industrial quality to the 20th century model of healthcare causes the contrasts between the two in structures, values and processes to appear. Simultaneously, the application of industrial quality and the resulting industrialization causes new images to appear that display the characteristics or images of the new model of 21st century healthcare. The 21st century model becomes clearer as the transformative aspects of industrialized quality are incorporated into healthcare organizations. The 21st century model is not fully realized during industrialization, but images of the future that appear during this period serve as guides in moving the organizations beyond industrialization to 21st century healthcare.

As healthcare organizations confront the 21st century, healthcare leaders and quality professionals face a number of challenges. The first challenge that leaders face is simply to recognize that their organizations must transition from a 20th century model of healthcare to a 21st century model of healthcare. There really is no way that the older models of healthcare organizations will survive in the 21st century. The massive changes occurring in the environment require that healthcare organizations change.

The second challenge is for healthcare leaders to recognize that this transformation requires the full application of the values, structures and processes of industrial quality in all areas of their organizations. The introduction of industrial quality begins the process of industrialization and, in fact, industrialization has already begun in almost every healthcare organization due to regulatory and payer requirements for data-driven improvements. To realize the benefits of industrialization that are necessary for the transition to 21st century healthcare requires healthcare leaders to promote the full implementation of industrial quality and industrialization into all aspects of their organizations. The promotion of industrialization by leaders converts the slow, incidental process that is already occurring into an accelerated intentional spread specifically designed to transform their organizations.

With the introduction of industrial quality and the spread of industrialization, healthcare leaders confront a third challenge. This third challenge requires leaders to recognize that industrialization is a phase in the transformation of healthcare organizations, but it is not the final stage. With industrialization, organizations recognize and begin movement along ten transitions that represent the progression from the older model of healthcare to the new 21st century model. Leaders need to be knowledgeable about the nature of these transitions and to observe and map the overall transformation of their organizations by assessing their progress in the ten transitions. Tracking the movement through the ten transitions serves as the basis for assessing the overall transformation of their organization and their readiness to meet the demands of the future. By developing strategies to accelerate movement along the continuums within the ten transitions, leaders facilitate the movement of their organizations toward 21st century healthcare.

The final challenge for leaders is to recognize the power of the emerging images and concepts of 21st century healthcare that appear through industrialization and their role as guides and motivators to facilitate organizational transformation. Successfully moving into the future requires the effective use of these images as generative metaphors within each of the ten transitions to inspire and motivate employees and to guide changes. Industrialization facilitates the initial movement of the organizations along the continuum in each of the ten transitions, but it is the images of the future within each transition that guide the organizational progression beyond industrialization and serve as the motivation for people to pursue the future. The vital role of leadership at all levels of the organization in this transformation is to understand that the industrialization process brings to light the ten transitions and initiates the movement along the continuum within each transition. In order to continue the progress along the continuum, however, leaders must recognize the images of 21st century healthcare that appear and articulate these visions of the future to motivate and guide the people involved.

The following sections discuss the ten transitions and provide transitional assessment charts for each one. These charts have two columns (identified as the 20th century and the 21st century) for the two categories for each transition that all healthcare organizations share. These categories identify the ends of the continuum within the specific transition. Under each of these categories are characteristics or descriptive phrases that the leadership in each organization identifies as characteristics for the 20th century and the 21st century in their organization. These form the images that help the organization and its employees recognize the beginning points of the transition and the end points for their transitions. Though the categories are the same, the specific characteristics may be different in different organizations because the organizations reflect the diversity of the different customs, values and practices of their communities. Several examples of organizational characteristics for each category are included in the transitional assessment charts for each of the transitions in the following sections to help leaders in identifying the characteristics in their organizations.

The characteristics that organizations identify become the beginning and end of the continuums for each of the transitions and identify the characteristics of the 20th century and the vision of the 21st century for their organizations. Using these characteristics, leaders have an important role in helping their organizations to assess their progress along the continuums and in articulating and promoting a clear vision of the future. The work of leadership within the transitions is to help their organizations to recognize the characteristics of the past that they are leaving behind and the vision of the future that they are pursuing as their organizations go through the transitions. The value of mapping movement along the continuum is in motivating the people in the organization to see the future in the characteristics of the transition and to actively work to move the organization toward its new future in healthcare.

Section 4.2, "Organizational Transitions," focuses on the transitions that reflect the foundational elements of structure, relationships, leadership and innovation of healthcare organizations. These transitions refer to the organization itself as it experiences the implementation of industrialization and advances toward the images of the 21st century.

Subsection 4.2.1, "Organizational Structure Transition: Hierarchy to Complex System," follows the often imperceptible shift from the 20th century model of hierarchical, bureaucratic organizational structure based on power and control to the 21st century complex system in which the centralized structure is minimized in favor of responsiveness to the needs of patients and customers at the point of service. The categories for this transition are the 20th century hierarchy and 21st century complex system.

Subsection 4.2.2, "Organizational Relationship Transition: Transactional to Emergent," tracks the movement from the 20th century transactional employee–employer relationship based on agreements of specific tasks and job descriptions and compensation to the future relationship in which the roles of employees are defined as they operationalize the mission and values of the organization through their interactions with each other and with their patients and customers. In healthcare organizations, the departmental bureaucracy lends itself to specific roles and activities associated with specific tasks and levels of compensation. In the future, the roles evolve within the context of interactions and the job descriptions focus on simpler rules and more flexibility for employees to respond to new developments. The categories for this transition are 20th century transactional relationship and the 21st century emergent relationship.

Subsection 4.2.3, "Leadership Transition: Control to Trust," represents a redefinition of leadership as it evolves from 20th to 21st century healthcare. In this transition, leadership moves from prediction, command and control to the new role of creating an environment of trust that inspires employees to make decisions and to express leadership within situations. As leaders recognize their own limitations to exercise control and predict outcomes in the new environment, the leadership role of authentically expressing the vision and values of the organization as guides and communicating trust in the people to actually create the organization through their activities becomes clearer. The categories for this transition are 20th century leadership control and 21st century leadership trust.

Finally, Subsection 4.2.4, "Innovation Transition: Centralized to Adaptive," maps the organizational shift from the 20th century model of centralized innovation as an expression of control by leadership to a new adaptive innovation model that emerges out of the work of the people as they solve problems and improve processes every day. The innovations that make 21st century organizations successful emerge from the creativity of many employees developing adaptive responses to diverse situations and interactions. Out of these many adaptive responses that are shared and replicated thousands of times, the organization evolves to better fit its environment. The categories for this transition are 20th century centralized innovation and 21st century adaptive innovation.

Section 4.3, "Process Transitions," addresses the ways organizations actually perform the work of delivering healthcare. The process transitions enable assessments of the operational aspects of healthcare production methods, service delivery, information systems and financing processes. As organizations evaluate the way work is performed from each of these perspectives, they bring to light the contrasts between the 20th century and the 21st century and create a path to the future.

Subsection 4.3.1, "Production Method Transition—Craftsman to Multidisciplinary Teams," follows the progression within healthcare from the 20th century craftsman model based on the autonomous physician to the multidisciplinary team of the 21st century in which groups share responsibility for the work and accountability for the care that is delivered. This transition represents a significant shift in the way physicians understand their roles and the way employees in organizations understand their responsibilities. The categories for this transition are 20th century craftsman and 21st century multidisciplinary teams.

Subsection 4.3.2, "Delivery System Transition: Hospital to Continuum of Care," represents the move from the hospital as the island of healthcare production in a sea of injury and illness to multiple delivery sites and services in a coordinated continuum of care. Information systems link a variety of services and service providers together to deliver the care the patients need at the time and place it is required and at the best cost. This transition recognizes the complexity of healthcare services and the ways in which the various

care providers coordinate their services to meet the needs
of patient-customers and communities. This transition assists
organizations in recognizing the move away from the hospital
as the production facility of healthcare to a continuum of care.
The categories for this transition are 20th century hospital and
21st century continuum of care.

Subsection 4.3.3, "Information System Transition: Isolation
to Network," maps a significant change between the past
and the future of healthcare. As healthcare organizations
move from paper medical records and the isolated computer
to enterprise network information systems, this transforms
the organization and increases the ability to coordinate and
deliver care effectively and efficiently. Staff access to real-time
information about patients, the delivery system and the ability
to communicate throughout the organization promote rapid
response to changes and the spread of innovation. This is a
key aspect of the changes in healthcare during industrialization and an important image of healthcare in the future. The
categories for the information system transition are 20th century isolation and 21st century network.

Finally, Subsection 4.3.4, "Financial Transition: Fee-for-
Service Financing to Consumer Health Financing," represents
a rebirth of the patient as a customer and an important part
of the financing of healthcare. The original payer for healthcare, the patient, was lost during the insurance age. As
patient-customers assume more responsibility for paying for
their healthcare as the government and the employers reduce
their roles, new financial services are needed to facilitate this
change. The contrast between the older model of employer
and governmental insurance payment mechanisms and the
future of patient-customers making decisions about care and
paying for care forms the basis for the transition. The categories for this transition are 20th century fee-for-service financing
and 21st century consumer health financing.

Section 4.4, "Cultural Transitions," tracks the cultural heart
of healthcare as industrialization reshapes it and new images

of the future appear. Of all the transitions, this touches the areas that are haunted most by the images of the 20th century and are perhaps the most difficult to change because of the strength of the original visions. Hidden within these transitions are important assumptions about the nature of healthcare in America. The images of healthcare that are appearing with industrialization require new images that challenge the prevailing sense of what is normal or right.

The shift from the autonomy of the physician to the integration of practitioners and patients into multidisciplinary teams of healthcare professionals is the focus of Subsection 4.4.1, "Professional Transition: Autonomy to Integration." This transition reflects a major shift in the actual practice of medicine. Sir Luke Fildes's painting of *The Doctor,* which was used so effectively in the lobbying efforts of the American Medical Association (AMA), still grips the consciousness of healthcare and the public. It is heroic and compassionate and moving in its humanity. It is also a vision of helplessness in the face of illness as the doctor watches passively to see the outcome for the sick child. The 21st century image of healthcare as a team of multidisciplinary professionals actively engaged in working with the patient to design the care that meets the patient's needs and desires contrasts sharply with the older image. The categories for this transition are 20th century professional autonomy and 21st century integration (Stevens 1998).

Subsection 4.4.2, "Metaphor Transition: Scientific Machine to Complex Adaptive System," is the metatransition or the overarching transition ignited by the fires of industrialization of healthcare. The 20th century metaphor of the scientific machine is pushed to its logical conclusion with industrialization, but in the process it gives birth to a new and very different image of the future as the complex adaptive system of 21st century healthcare. It is in this metatransition that the effects of industrialization are fully realized—as well as its limitations. Industrialization of healthcare is the culmination of the work that was begun at the start of the 20th century with scientific management and bureaucracy but left unfinished until the introduction of industrial quality. The scientific machine image of healthcare organizations was never realized in the past because it was undermined by the professionalization of the physician and the structuring of healthcare around this craftsman model throughout the 20th century. In the metaphor transition, the carefully designed and assembled machine that forms an important image of industrialization and is the force behind the movement of healthcare from the 20th to the 21st century fades as the image of the complex adaptive system emerges in the transition to the 21st century. The categories for this transition are 20th century scientific machine and 21st century complex adaptive system.

The final section, "The Transition Scorecard and Transition Progress Scale," provides the means for actually measuring the progress of healthcare organizations in their movement through the transitions. Each of the transitions has a comparative chart that includes the categories as separate columns that contrast the 20th and 21st century models. The sums from each of the columns in the individual transitions flow up to a larger scorecard that brings all ten categories together. There is a final score that identifies the progression of the organization toward the 21st century as the measure of the movement through the transitions.

4.2 Organizational Transitions

Organizational transitions reflect the foundational elements of structure, relationships, leadership and innovation of healthcare organizations. These transitions address the aspects of the organization that refer to the ways the organization experiences the implementation of industrialization and advances toward the images of the 21st century.

4.2.1 Organizational Structure Transition: Hierarchy to Complex System

The first of the organizational transitions is the organizational structure transition. The 20th century column is designated as "hierarchy." The 21st century column is "complex system." The focus of this transition is the progress of healthcare organizations as they move along the continuum from a hierarchical structure to a complex system structure. Identifying characteristics in your organization that align with a hierarchical structure or a complex system structure and describing them in the appropriate column provide the basis for assessing the progress of your organization as it moves from the 20th century model to the 21st century model of healthcare.

The 20th century hierarchy column refers to the traditional way in which healthcare organizations structured the bureaucracy of departments and reporting relationships in the 20th century. Based on the scientific machine view of management and organizations, all of the departments and management positions within the bureaucracy in the organization align in reporting relationships that promote central leadership command, information flow from the top and resources control. From the top of the organization to the bottom, each position and each person has a reporting relationship that is clearly defined. The ability of the individual to control organizational resources and to command organizational activities is defined by the position the individual holds and the positions that report to him or her throughout the organization from the CEO down. In addition to the control of resources and the command over activities, the hierarchy in place in 20th century organizations serves as the primary channel for the flow of organizational information, with the greatest access to information held by the positions with the most power at the top of the organization and the least access by those in the lowest positions with the least power.

The 21st century complex system is the organizational structure of the future and the image that healthcare organizations work to define and use as a guide as they move along the continuum of the organizational structure transition. This organizational structure originates out of the change in the flow of information that results from the implementation of electronic information systems. Rather than conceiving of the structure of the organization as an expression of positional authority and accountability, the complex system structure arises out of the connections between individuals, departments, functions and even areas outside the healthcare organizations linked by information systems and engaged in the rapid exchange of information. As individuals throughout the organization—not just at the top—share information in the course of their day and in response to their needs in performing work, the complex system forms and functions.

The organizational structure transition describes the characteristics that contrast the hierarchy of the 20th century and the complex system of the 21st century. Connections facilitated by increasingly sophisticated information systems undermine the hierarchy based on positions and power. The vertical structure of hierarchy no longer serves to effectively describe the work as the focus shifts to multidirectional linking of functions and groups that share information in real time and coordinate activities with less and less direction from the top, central leadership. The emphasis is on connections and communications and less on positional power and titles and a vertically defined hierarchy.

The organizational structure transition assessment chart (Figure 4.1) is a way for leaders to assess the transition within their organizations from the 20th century hierarchy to the 21st century complex system. The characteristics for each of these models are presented as examples, but will differ for each organization depending on a variety of factors. The characteristics identified with the 20th century under the organization structure transition in the chart capture the bureaucratic and hierarchical nature that characterizes the scientific machine understanding of 20th century healthcare

20th Century Hierarchy Characteristics	Points (neg.)	21st Century Complex System Characteristics	Points (pos.)
Organizational chart describes positional authority and accountability		Organizational system depiction used in place of organizational chart	
Information flow follows vertical power alignment in the organizational chart		Information flows freely across connections throughout the system	
Total (record on scorecard)		Total (record on scorecard)	

Figure 4.1   Organizational structure transition assessment chart.

organizations. Since this structure and these characteristics are associated with a 20th century understanding of healthcare organizations, their continuance indicates a lack of progress toward the 21st century. The characteristics associated with the 21st century complex system are a fluid, dynamic organizational structure in which connections that facilitate real-time information flow and rapid response form the basis for the way in which the organization is structured and operates. Recognizing that it is a powerful metaphor for the organization, the characteristics of your organizational chart provide a tool for you to use in assessing the progress your organization is making in moving from the 20th century hierarchy to the 21st century complex system.

The common usage and familiarity of the organization chart make it difficult for most people to recognize that it is a powerful symbol for fundamental beliefs that underlie the structure and operation of healthcare organizations. The lines

and boxes that present specific positions and lines of accountability and communication in the organization chart function
the same way as lines in the diagram of a mechanical device
in portraying the connections in the machine. By placing the
most powerful titles and boxes at the top of the chart and less
powerful boxes and titles lower on the chart, the machinery
of the organization is displayed in terms of how it expects
to accomplish its purposes. The boxes at the top of the chart
communicate the directions and plans down through the
lower boxes along the lines on the chart. The lower boxes
direct everyone not pictured on the chart and then report
what was accomplished back to the top of the chart. The
machine is designed to transmit commands down through the
hierarchy and for the results of operations to be submitted up
through the hierarchy. The vertical directions of command and
control and communication are depicted and the lack of connections between the vertical silos is clear.

The characteristics in the 21st century complex system column contrast with the 20th century hierarchy column. Rather
than an organizational chart designed to depict power, control
and reporting structures, organizations that think of themselves as complex systems find ways to recognize their complexity and the connections that actually function within the
organization. There are a variety of ways that this metaphor
can be depicted graphically, but it works against the view that
there are columns of influence and power and works toward
the links that connect the complex system together. Service
lines and matrix diagrams have been used in various industries, but healthcare as a service provider that incorporates
professionals at all levels of the process needs to imagine a
more creative image that fully depicts its complexity and unity
as a system. Leadership is a function of these connections, but
the diagram should present a fluid, dynamic organizational
structure in which connections that facilitate real-time information flow and rapid response form the basis for the way

in which the organization is structured and operates. As a complex system in which changes occur rapidly, the diagram needs to offer a sense of the way the processes and decisions take place as quickly as possible at the point of service with minimal central leadership control. Sophisticated information systems facilitate the rapid changes and maintain the communications that enable resources to move quickly when they are needed. It is in this environment that the demands of 21st century healthcare overwhelm the structures of the 20th century organizational chart and require that they change or otherwise the organization will fail. This is the motivation for movement along the continuum of the organizational structure transition (Wheatley 1992; Zimmerman, Plsek and Lindberg 2001; Uhl-Bien and McKelvey 2008; Crowell 2011; Zimmerman 2011).

4.2.2 Organizational Relationship Transition: Transactional to Emergent

The second organizational transition is the organizational relationship transition. The 20th century column is designated as "transactional relationships." The 21st century column is "emergent relationships." The focus of this transition is the progress of healthcare organizations as they move along the continuum from transactional employer–employee relationships to emergent relationships. Identifying characteristics in your organization that align with the transactional or the emergent relationships and describing them in the appropriate column provide the basis for assessing the progress of your organization as it moves from the 20th century model to the 21st century model of healthcare.

In the organizational relationship transition, the assessment focuses on the relationship between the organization and the people who work there. The culture of organizations arises out of a variety of sources and influences and reflects the values of the society and the ideas associated with the management philosophy. In the 20th century, the relationships within the typical bureaucratic organizations were defined on the basis of a transaction or agreement in which the worker negotiated with the organization for specific compensation in exchange for specific labor. The terms of the agreement in the job description and in the salary or hourly rate of pay and benefits offered for the work provided the basis for the relationship between the worker and the healthcare organization.

In the 21st century complex system structure, a new relationship is needed. No longer is it sufficient for the worker to agree to simply perform certain tasks in exchange for specific wages. The 21st century healthcare organization requires employees to engage in critical thinking and creativity as they translate the culture of the organization into their work. In exchange, the employees look to management to participate in the relationship through the development of a mission and vision and values that the employee finds worthwhile and that management consistently models. It is in this context that the continuum of the organizational relationship transition is used to evaluate progress toward 21st century healthcare.

The organizational relationship transition assessment chart (Figure 4.2) is a way for leaders to assess the transition within their organizations from the 20th century transactional relationship to the 21st century emergent relationship. The characteristics for each of these models are presented as examples, but the characteristics and number of characteristics will differ depending on the complexity of the design of the organization. The characteristics identified with the 20th century transactional relationship in the chart reflect the structure of the agreements that characterized the transactional nature of the relationship between the organization and the workers in the 20th century healthcare bureaucracy. The characteristics associated with the 21st century emergent relationship focus on the way in which the people create the relationship with the organization through their activities that operationalize the mission

20th Century Transactional Relationships Characteristics	Points (neg.)	21st Century Emergent Relationships Characteristics	Points (pos.)
Job descriptions describe specific work tasks only		Job description describes role of mission and values in work	
Task-oriented work evaluations		Mission and values-oriented work evaluations	
Total (record on scorecard)		Total (record on scorecard)	

Figure 4.2 Organizational relationship transition assessment chart.

and vision and values. As organizations assess their progress from the characteristics of the formal, limited understanding of a transactional relationship to the characteristics of a more fluid and dynamic relationship of the future, they demonstrate progress along the continuum toward the 21st century.

In the 20th century transactional relationship the emphasis is on the way in which the employee and the organization establish the relationship. The basis for the relationship is the document in which the job description and the compensation are defined and the expectations of the organization and the worker are clearly defined. Given this foundation for the relationship, the worker's contributions to the organization are limited to the work and to the specific expectations of the job requirements. The transactional agreement heightens the role of management as defining, designing and overseeing the work and the worker as completing tasks. This arrangement strengthens the hierarchical structure within which it flourishes by limiting access to information, placing the emphasis of fulfilling specific tasks and job requirements and establishing the senior leadership and management as holding the workers accountable for fulfilling their requirements (Burns 1978).

In the 21st century emergent relationship, the emphasis is on healthcare organizations as a complex system of relationships that are contingent on individual initiative and understanding of the purpose and goals of the organization. As information systems accelerate the rate of information flow on a moment-by-moment basis, the individual is confronted with a number of situations in which independent decision making is required. In this context, the culture of the organization is much more an understanding of the goals and values than it is the direction from a centralized leadership group. The ability of individuals and groups to shape their decisions and activities within simple rules derived from the values and mission of the organization are key characteristics of this organizational structure. Organizational culture emerges within the context of multiple relationships adapting the common mission, vision and values to everyday situations. Goals and responsibilities emerge as the system adapts to the environment, and functions and roles emerge in response to system needs. The relationships that exist within the organization and with the customers and communities outside the organization emerge through the interactions that occur every day. As individuals and groups of employees interact together and with people outside of the organization, they establish and build and shape the relationships that actually define the organization. The organization is not a building and it is not a piece of paper; rather, it is created out of the interactions that occur in each encounter and it comes to life at these points of contact.

In looking at the nature of 21st century healthcare as a complex system, the key elements that govern the relationship between employee and management are bound up in the mission, vision and values. The compensation and evaluations of employees reflect the ability of employees to operationalize the culture of the organization in their work and the consistency of leadership in expressing these values. In this way, the

21st century healthcare organization emerges not as a document or as a building but rather as a living, dynamic entity adapting to a constantly changing environment in which people realize their potential through meaningful and creative interactions supported by values-based and engaged authentic leadership (Crowell 2011; Wheatley 1992).

4.2.3 Leadership Transition: Control to Trust

The third organizational transition is the leadership transition. The 20th century column is designated as "control." The 21st century column is labeled "trust." The focus of this transition is the progress of healthcare organizations as they move along the continuum from leadership that controls and directs to a leadership that trusts and empowers. Identifying characteristics in your organization that align with a controlling leadership or a trusting and empowering leadership and describing them in the appropriate column provide the basis for assessing the progress of your organization as it moves from the 20th century model to the 21st century model of healthcare.

In the leadership transition, the 20th century model of healthcare leadership reflects the patriarchal and authoritarian leadership as the initial pole of the continuum. This leadership model emphasizes control and command, the monitoring of resources and judging of work with minimal participation by the employees in the decisions associated with their roles. This form of leadership is consistent with the professional autonomy of the physician and the emerging scientific management of the hospital that began in the early 20th century and dominated healthcare through most of the century. The leader, whether administrative or medical, makes decisions and the organization is structured to follow these decisions. Leadership is defined by title and position, financial control and decision-making power.

The 21st century view of leadership evolving in healthcare offers a very different perspective. The leadership of the future is less defined by title and position and more by the ability and willingness of individuals to respond to changes and exercise leadership in the moment that it is needed and where it is needed. In this view, leadership emerges as it is needed and shifts from person to person and place to place in response to rapid changes that require responses in real time. There are still roles with defined responsibilities for oversight and management of resources, but the actual exercise of leadership is seen as a system function rather than a position or a set of prerogatives. System leadership promotes coordination through the communication of a common mission, vision, values and language. Leadership interactions are characterized by relational transparency and trust (Wheatley 1992; Uhl-Bien and McKelvey 2008; Crowell 2011).

The leadership transition assessment chart (Figure 4.3) is a way for leaders to assess the transition within their organizations from 20th century leadership control to the 21st century leadership trust. The characteristics for each of these models

20th Century Leadership Control Characteristics	Points (neg.)	21st Century Leadership Trust Characteristics	Points (pos.)
Organizational chart defines scope of control for positions		Broad definition of leadership encourages individuals to take initiative at all levels	
Leadership positions control work throughout organization		Employee leadership expressly encouraged by senior leaders	
Total (record on scorecard)		Total (record on scorecard)	

Figure 4.3   Leadership transition assessment chart.

are presented as examples, but the characteristics and number of characteristics will differ depending on the complexity of the design of the organization. The 20th century leadership control in the chart characterizes the role of leadership as controlling and commanding the operations and the activities of employees within the organization in a manner consistent with the 20th century scientific machine bureaucracy. The characteristics associated with the 21st century leadership trust focus on the nature of leadership redefined as situational and functional rather than positional and arbitrary. The rapid changes and constant flow of information in the 21st century require a framework of trust in which employees are able to function as leaders and make decisions based on clear understanding of the mission and vision and simple rules without constant reference back to position authority. As organizations assess their progress from the characteristics of leadership as command and control exercised as positional authority to the characteristics of leadership as situational and functional response by anyone who is able to address the needs of the organization or the customers, the organization demonstrates progress along the continuum toward the 21st century.

The 20th century leadership control model in healthcare organizations works off the hierarchical structure in which leadership is clearly defined by the position the person holds and the positions and departments in the bureaucracy that are subordinate to that position. It is designed to be a very clear connection between superior and inferior positions and the responsibilities exercised by each in the structure. This structure follows the concept of a bureaucracy as designed for efficiency and control and to facilitate the communication from the positions at the top of the organization to the operational positions and departments at the bottom. Healthcare organizations experience the effects of positional power differently from most other organizations due to the presence of physicians who have their own symbols of power and prerogatives that often exceed those associated with nonclinical positional power. Nonetheless, positional power and control is still part of American healthcare organizations on the bureaucratic side. In many organizations, individuals in positions of power exercise substantial control over the operation of the organization, in the access to resources, in the prerogatives assigned to the titles, in substantial bonuses, preferential office and parking and in options for conferences and administrative assistance. Many of these positions are valuable primarily because they extend the authority and control of senior leadership down into the organization and facilitate the reporting up from operational positions to the central leadership.

In the 21st century leadership column, the role of leadership shifts from control to trust. This shift is not because individuals in positions of power want to give up their control. The change represents the reality of healthcare organizations as complex systems. The speed of the changes and the number of decisions that must be made each day exceed the ability of the people in positions of power to respond effectively. Even monitoring the activities in the system is daunting when thousands of contacts and interactions may occur every day. Leadership must be redefined to fit this new structure and the definition of leadership must be broadened to encompass the decisions made by employees at every level. In the speed of the activities of the network and the connectivity of the system in which information flows continuously, the positions of power can no longer actively control and manage the work as they did before. Their work in this environment is to create relationships of trust with employees built on shared goals and the consistent application of values.

Employees in this environment are required to make decisions quickly that affect many types of customers. In making these decisions, they express leadership as a part of their work. In working with fellow employees and entities outside the organization, they demonstrate leadership as the need arises by coordinating with other people and arranging responses that resolve issues. They need guidance to make these decisions and a framework of simple rules to demonstrate leadership in a way that is consistent with the organization as a whole. They also need to know that they have the support of the organization in making these decisions and to trust that positions of power will support decisions that are based on the mission, the goals and the values of the organization. It is in creating a new definition of leadership based on trust rather than on control that the new organization is able to draw on the abilities of all the employees to exercise leadership and make decisions. This new approach is based on the need of the system to respond quickly while at the same time maintaining consistency in the responses throughout the system (Burns 1978; Lindberg, Nash and Lindberg 2008; Crowell 2011).

4.2.4 Innovation Transition: Centralized to Adaptive

The fourth and final organizational transition is the innovation transition. The 20th century column is designated as "centralized innovation." The 21st century column is "adaptive innovation." The focus of this transition is the progress of healthcare organizations as they move along the continuum from centralized innovation controlled by the hierarchical leadership to adaptive innovation that emerges from the workers as the organization responds to internal and environmental changes. Identifying characteristics in your organization that align with a centralized innovation or adaptive innovation and describing them in the appropriate column provide the basis for assessing the progress of your organization as it moves from the 20th century model to the 21st century model of healthcare.

Scientific management in 20th century healthcare organization, like 20th century manufacturing, placed the responsibility for innovation on management rather than on the workers. Physicians designed and managed the delivery of care and the hospital bureaucracy designed and managed the support services. Nurses and other staff took orders and were rewarded for promptness and efficiency in carrying out orders. Ideas originated in the upper portion of the organizational chart in the centralized positions of power. Initiatives for change were generated by these positions because they enjoyed access to system information and had the authority to require changes associated with the innovations.

In the 21st century, innovation becomes an ongoing event as information flows throughout the organization and adaptive responses are needed to manage new developments. There is not enough time to wait for the central positions to come up with new ideas when the organization and environment are rapidly changing and patients and practitioners need innovative responses to adapt to change on a daily basis. Continuous, incremental innovation occurs throughout the organization. Innovation is encouraged at the point of service or care and is supported with resources. In evaluating an organization's place on the continuum between centralized innovation and adaptive change, the key markers will be the ability of staff at the interface of the organization with patients, customers and the community to develop and implement ideas. The availability of resources and support for testing new ideas at the point of care and staff having time to develop ideas indicate progress on the continuum.

The innovation transition assessment chart (Figure 4.4) is a way for leaders to assess the transition within their organizations from the 20th century centralized innovation to the 21st century adaptive innovation. The characteristics for each of these models are presented as examples, but the characteristics and number of characteristics will differ depending on the complexity of the design of the organization. The characteristics identified with the 20th century centralized innovation in the chart focus on the role of leadership as controlling the development, analysis and implementation of innovation. Since innovation by nature challenges the command and control of 20th century bureaucracy, it is clearly in the interests of the

20th Century Centralized Innovation Characteristics	Points (neg.)	21st Century Adaptive Innovation Characteristics	Points (pos.)
Central leadership dictates new services and processes		Innovation emerges from employees where work is performed	
Innovation discouraged outside central leadership		Adaptive innovation expressly encouraged at the point where work is performed	
Total (record on scorecard)		Total (record on scorecard)	

Figure 4.4   Innovation transition assessment chart.

individuals with positional authority to maintain a very tight control on the way innovation occurs. This is consistent with the 20th century view of the healthcare environment changing only slowly. The characteristics associated with the 21st century adaptive innovation highlight the new organizational realities of rapid change in the course of daily work. Adaptive innovation occurs in response to changes in the environment and in the organization on a frequent basis and reflects the 21st century view of change as normal and creative adaptation as part of the work. The rapid changes and constant flow of information in the 21st century require a framework within which innovation can occur, be tested and be implemented quickly while maintaining the necessary elements of standardization to ensure quality. As organizations assess their progress from the characteristics of the restrictive, formalized innovation to the characteristics of adaptive innovation that is built into the work, the organization demonstrates progress along the continuum toward the 21st century.

In the 20th century centralized innovation model, the hierarchical structure of the organizational chart of 20th century healthcare organizations provides a clear image of the way in which positions relate and information flows. It also provides a meaningful representation of the way ideas are generated in this organizational structure. The top of the organizational chart and the positions of power are the locus of control out of which innovation is expected to arise for the organization. The information necessary to recognize the need for innovation is at the top of the organization and it is at this level that the structures and the work are defined and designed. At this level, information from all the areas that may be affected by the innovation can be brought together and assessed, and the way in which the innovation may affect the organization can be evaluated. It is also at this level that the links between the bureaucracy and the medical staff within the 20th century healthcare organization are most clearly seen and able to be incorporated into any type of innovation that may affect the physicians. For the 20th century healthcare organization, innovation is problematic and the management of it to ensure that it does not interfere with the work and structure of the organization is a priority for the top leadership. Innovation in and of itself is not viewed as an essential value to the future of the organization, because the future of the organization is perceived to be like the past. Maintaining the stability of the work processes is considered much more valuable than innovation. Innovation is carefully managed by the leadership to prevent it from spreading spontaneously and disrupting the existing processes. When innovation is needed and viewed as something the organization must do, the leaders carefully control the development and implementation to prevent disruption of the status quo. The change is packaged to fit within the current structure to maintain the image of stability and to minimize disruptions.

In 21st century adaptive innovation, the role of innovation in the future of healthcare and its role in the survival of organizations becomes clearer as the importance of innovation that flows out of the activities of the organization and interaction of the organization with the environment is recognized. It is not innovation for the sake of innovation or the whim of a powerful individual, but it is rather an adaptive response to a constantly changing environment and the internal dynamics within the organization. The sources of innovation and the ability of the organization to absorb innovation are critically important to the way innovation arises and the way it spreads. Innovation is embraced and encouraged because it is viewed as the way in which the organization discovers the best fit with the environment. The source of the innovation is unimportant. The key is being able to recognize the innovation that has potential benefit and opening channels for it to move through the organization. In the 21st century healthcare organization, innovation arises naturally out of the dynamic environment within which the organization functions. It is adaptive innovation because it is born of the need that emerges from the interface of the organization with the changing environment (Morgan 2006).

The challenge for the 21st century healthcare organizations is to accommodate this naturally occurring response and harness the energy and creative drive. The most important aspect of the incorporation of adaptive innovation into healthcare organizations is the recognition that innovation arises out of the work rather than as a function of positional leadership. Without understanding that new ideas develop wherever work is performed, the organization will not be able to recognize innovation when it occurs and will not be able to absorb and benefit from it. Creating the channels to guide new ideas emerging from the work is the structural imperative that 21st century organizations must address to manage this creative impulse.

The spread of innovation requires the organization to find ways to promote communication between all areas. This means creating new spaces for meetings and new opportunities for individuals and groups to interact. It also means making resources available to encourage efforts to trial innovation with the expectations that these trials may not work. The willingness to make it easy for resources to be applied to innovative ideas supports innovation itself and promotes the spread of new ideas. It also provides the organization with the means for testing and refining new ideas that are promising.

Finally, the judgment of innovation must move from the test of consistency with the status quo to the test of fulfilling the mission, vision and values of the organization. Innovation by definition will be inconsistent with the status quo and difficult for the existing organization to absorb. Using the mission as the basis for evaluating new ideas and for judging the success of innovation provides the flexibility and foundation for innovation to move beyond the existing reality and to open the way to a new approach that takes the organization to a higher level.

4.3 Process Transitions

The process transitions from the 20th century healthcare model to the 21st century model represent significant changes in the processes that produce healthcare. These processes involve the production of healthcare as it moves from the independent craftsman practitioner in the small community to the multidisciplinary team that is able to bring all the knowledge and expertise of healthcare to bear in accomplishing the goals of the patient. The delivery system of the 20th century transitions from the fortress-like hospital sitting majestically within the community to the continuum of healthcare delivery that is architecturally less dominating but more efficient and effective in meeting the needs of the patient. Information systems become the nervous system and circulatory system as they move from isolation based on individual computer programs to networks in systems that feed the energy of information to all parts of the healthcare network. And the final element of the process transition is the redesign of the financial system from the fee-for-service concept that promotes the use of technology and large buildings to consumer health financing that is focused on enabling the patient to obtain and to pay for care wherever it is delivered in the healthcare system.

4.3.1 Production Method Transition: Craftsman to Multidisciplinary Teams

The first of the process transitions is the production method transition. The 20th century column is designated as "craftsman." The 21st century column is "multidisciplinary team." The focus of this transition is on the progress of healthcare organizations as they move along the continuum from the craftsman production built around the individual physician to the multidisciplinary team. Identifying characteristics in your organization that align with the individual physicians or multidisciplinary team production and describing them in the appropriate column provide the basis for assessing the progress that your organization is making as it moves from the 20th century model to the 21st century model of healthcare.

American healthcare in the 18th century and much of the 19th century consisted of people in small towns sharing knowledge and experience to benefit each other. In this craftsman model of healthcare, individuals with knowledge or experience delivered care to other people in the same way that a carpenter prepared a chair for a customer. The quality and the efficacy of the healthcare were directly related to the ability of the individual physician or town herbalist. If the outcomes were good more often than not, then the people would seek out the service of the local care provider the same way they would those of any other craftsman.

Due to the efforts of the AMA and the specialization of physicians around new technology and surgery, the role of the physician as a professional developed. This role eclipsed the efforts of others to participate in the care of patients except in subservience to the physicians. This process was institutionalized through licensure to prescribe and write orders and membership in the medical staff of local hospitals. This 20th century model places all of the responsibility for the processes of care as well as the prerogatives of care on the physician.

With the expansion of information systems as well as the rapid growth of healthcare research and knowledge, the physician is no longer able to know all that is known or needs to be known to care for patients. As physicians have become employees of health systems and as new specialties have developed involving nonphysicians, multidisciplinary teams developed in healthcare organizations. Processes and outcomes measures are shared by groups of care providers from various disciplines. Group decision making on care delivery and the ability to modify care in response to changes without the direct involvement of the physician represent moves on the continuum toward a broader care team approach.

The production method transition assessment chart (Figure 4.5) is a way for leaders to assess the transition within their organizations from the 20th century craftsman production to the 21st century multidisciplinary team. The characteristics for each of these models are presented as examples, but the characteristics and number of characteristics will differ depending on the complexity and the design of the organization. The characteristics identified with the 20th century craftsman production in the chart point toward the dominance of the individual physician in the work of hospitals and healthcare in general during the 20th century. As craftsmen supported by licensure and other regulatory requirements and the voice of the hospital medical staff in the design of work flows, the individual physicians shaped much of the work of

20th Century Craftsman Characteristics	Points (neg.)	21st Century Multidisciplinary Team Characteristics	Points (pos.)
Independent physician in solo practice requires clearance of all care of his patients		Physician and other professionals part of multidisciplinary team	
Physician directs all aspects of care to achieve physician's goals.		Care based on patient goals	
Total (record on scorecard)		Total (record on scorecard)	

Figure 4.5   Production method transition assessment chart.

healthcare around personal preferences and as an extension of their office practices. The characteristics associated with the 21st century multidisciplinary team acknowledge the essential role of the physician, but place it within the context of a team consisting of multiple disciplines that are actually focused on the patient rather than the physician in the design of the work. This shift in the production method of healthcare creates a significant change in the way healthcare is provided to the patient and the way in which responsibility for the care shifts to the team rather than resting on the individual physician. Through this change in production, physicians focus on those aspects of care associated with their expertise and the other disciplines in the team bring their special knowledge and skills to the care process. As organizations assess their progress from the characteristics of the craftsman physician model to the characteristics of multidisciplinary teams, the organization demonstrates progress along the continuum toward the 21st century.

In the 20th century craftsman production model, the emphasis is on the art of medicine rather than the science. In 20th century healthcare organizations, the physician is viewed as a scientist in terms of training and knowledge, but as a craftsman in terms of the application of that knowledge to the individual patient. Each patient is unique and the physician is expected to formulate a unique understanding and plan of care for each individual. It is within this context that the 20th century physician is best understood as the initial starting point for this transition. The independent physician as a craftsman is the model for the structure and operation of 20th century healthcare delivery. The physician working solo or in a small joint practice with another physician designs and manages all aspects of the operation of the medical office. With only the state licensing board and the local hospital playing a role in the work of the physician, the credentials of training, licensure and medical staff membership are the basis for qualifying to practice medicine.

The independent physician holds a unique position in the community. The level of trust necessary for the physician to provide care to patients means that people in the community view the physician on the same level as other highly trained professionals such as clergy and attorneys. In directing all aspects of patient care, the physician is seen as personally responsible for the recovery of patients and for saving lives. The care of the patient is delivered by the physician and the physician defines for the patient the goals of care. This becomes the ultimate basis for determining the quality of care since there is no other oversight.

Finally, it is the physicians in the community that create the processes of care through their interactions with patients and the local hospital. Physicians control all care through their orders, and this gives the physicians control over the way care is delivered. The way physicians write orders, document care, conduct rounds on their patients and interact with hospital staff determines the way that care is delivered. In writing orders, the physicians initiate care that can cost hundreds of thousands of dollars and require extensive engagement of hospital resources. The physician, however, is not responsible for the costs or guaranteeing the outcomes of these processes.

The 21st century multidisciplinary team model represents a result of healthcare passing through industrialization and into the 21st century model. The independent physician in a solo practice is the rarity rather than the rule. Following major shifts in healthcare regulations, insurance requirements, technological advances and patient demands, physicians in the new era are likely to be in a large practice or to be employed by a health system. Pulling back the curtain to reveal the complexity and the breadth of healthcare's multidisciplinary reality is the focus of the 21st century multidisciplinary team as the end point of the production method continuum. Recognizing the continuing major role of the physician but placing it within the context of the multidisciplinary team creates a more efficient and more effective delivery system and a more creative approach to healthcare. This opens up the team dynamic so that each professional is able to contribute and is not overshadowed by another. It also recognizes that it is the patient who is setting the goals of care rather than the physician. Within the team each professional plays a role and takes responsibility for contributing to the fulfillment of the patient's goals for care.

The multidisciplinary healthcare team of the 21st century takes as its starting point the patient's goals, and this becomes the focus as members of each discipline work with the patient and with each other to develop the plan of care. By reducing the focus on an individual or a particular discipline, the team is able to redirect the attention of the entire team to the patient. This focus on the patient enables the team to blend their views and skills and goals into a common purpose that serves the patient.

The quality of care is a team product rather than the results of one person's efforts, and the team is responsible for developing the plan of care and partnering with the patient to carry it out. The team of professionals brings their various skills and talents to the task of understanding the needs and desires of the patient and building a plan to achieve the goals of the patient. They hold each other accountable for the quality of their work and the integrity of their commitment to the patient. The team as a team forms around the patient through this unique blending of personal and professional contributions and produces the high-quality healthcare that is the vision of the 21st century.

4.3.2 Delivery System Transition: Hospital to Continuum of Care

The second of the process transitions is the delivery system transition. The 20th century column is designated as "hospital." The 21st century column is "continuum of care." The focus of this transition is the progress of healthcare organizations as they move along the continuum from the isolated hospital healthcare delivery system to the continuum-of-care delivery system. Identifying characteristics in your organization that align with an isolated hospital or a continuum-of-care delivery system and describing them in the appropriate column provide the basis for assessing the progress that your organization is making as it moves from the 20th century model to the 21st century model of healthcare.

A hallmark of 20th century healthcare was the impressive but isolated hospital that served as the healthcare factory of the community. All the resources to deliver the latest healthcare services were in the hospital along with the specialists. In the community, the local physicians were on the medical staff of the hospital and admitted and cared for their patients in that hospital. It was independent and a cherished symbol of community pride. Services in hospitals were developed and delivered without reference to a continuum of care since most patients went home after discharge to care provided by family or private-duty nursing. Transfers of patients were managed as individual transactions.

In the 21st century, the hospital is rapidly becoming only one of a number of stops on the continuum of care that begins with primary and preventive care and continues through outpatient and inpatient acute care to a wide variety of post-acute-care in facilities or in the home. The growth of care delivery along a continuum is still in the developmental stages but is rapidly developing in response to financial and societal pressures. Service delivery is a seamless continuum of care moving through levels of acuity based on patient need. System-based outcomes and payments are shared along the continuum. Assessing progress in the development of the continuum of care is the basis for the delivery system transition.

The delivery system transition assessment chart (Figure 4.6) is a way for leaders to assess the transition within their organizations from the 20th century hospital to the 21st century

20th Century Hospital Characteristics	Points (neg.)	21st Century Continuum of Care Characteristics	Points (pos.)
Routine care still requires hospital visit		Routine care available in multiple sites outside hospital	
Hospital has limited relationships with or connections to other care agencies		Strong links across the continuum of care between hospital and other agencies	
Total (record on scorecard)		Total (record on scorecard)	

Figure 4.6   Delivery system transition assessment chart.

continuum of care. The characteristics for each of these models are presented as examples, but the characteristics and number of characteristics will differ depending on the complexity and the design of the organization. The characteristics identified with the 20th century delivery system hospital are the view that only the hospital is the place where healthcare is delivered. The hospital may receive or discharge patients to other institutions or agencies, but the hospital views itself and is viewed by others as the unique place where healthcare occurs. The characteristics associated with the 21st century continuum of care focus on the reality that the healthcare delivery system has experienced extensive diversification in terms of agencies and services. The hospital is only one component of the healthcare continuum of care and is a part of the continuum to be used only when absolutely necessary due to costs and the design of services for high-acuity patients. As organizations assess their progress from the characteristics of delivery system as hospital to the characteristics of a continuum of care, the organization demonstrates progress along the continuum toward the 21st century.

In the 20th century hospital, the reality is the lack of a system of care and the isolation that characterized the physician and the hospital. The physician was the lone person controlling the delivery of healthcare in the 20th century and the hospital emerged as the focal point of the delivery system because it was the place where physicians had the technology and support to deliver care. These two images of the physician and the hospital represent 20th century American healthcare and the way patients perceived healthcare during the century. The hospital in the 20th century delivery of healthcare is the central focus of care and the hope of the community that modern, technologically advanced care will be available whenever it is needed. This modern healthcare production facility is the most visible and symbolic representation of the community's aspirations for good health and relief from pain, but it is not the entirety of a system of care. It sits in glorious isolation disconnected from the multiple other care providers scattered around it that operate on their own in delivering care. Within the walls of the hospital the germ of a system exists in the relationships and communications between the physicians and other disciplines, but this does not reach out into the community. The hospital provides a variety of services for the benefit of patients while they are in the hospital, but does not stretch this coordination and management outside the walls of the hospital and into creating a system of care in the community. This isolation is reinforced by the payment processes within the hospital. This payment process incorporates the services delivered by the hospital and physician but does not extend beyond the walls to other providers. The orders of the physician that apply only to the hospital care play a significant role in reinforcing the isolation. The documentation in the medical record restricts access to information to those who are in the hospital and does not provide access outside the hospital. This documentation becomes the focal point of understanding the lack of a system focus for 20th century hospital care. There is little connection or coordination between the hospital and the community providers that could be characterized as a system of care between providers and services.

The 21st century continuum of care describes a healthcare delivery system built on the connectivity and interdependence of the organizations and services that deliver care at different levels of acuity to meet the diverse needs of individuals. Rather than pieces of a puzzle scattered around the community, the continuum of care in the 21st century fits together to deliver the services when the patient needs them and in the most effective and efficient way. This configuration is very different from the hospital-centric 20th century model that required the patient and the individual practitioner to piece together individual services to meet the patient's needs. In the 21st century, the system is designed as a system with multiple access points open to the patient. With guidance, patients are able to select and access services that meet their needs. As patients utilize the services, the system monitors the points of contact and maintains the documentation so that the professionals involved in the care are able to coordinate the care and respond more effectively to the patients' needs in a more efficient and less costly manner. A vitally important distinction between the 20th century and 21st century healthcare systems is the development and operation of a vast network of service agencies and providers that deliver care to the patients in the community. In the 20th century, the hospital stood alone and other agencies clustered around it but were not connected to it. In the 21st century, the hospital has a leadership role in the creation, operations and maintenance of the continuum of care through a network of agreements and sharing of information. It provides much of the expertise, the infrastructure and the resources for managing the system. The hospital's staff monitors the actual movement of patient-customers in the system and their utilization of the resources. The hospital, however, requires the cooperation of multiple agencies in order to provide patients in the 21st century with the support and guidance they need to access the system, obtain services that they need and pay for those services through appropriate insurance arrangements. For healthcare organizations, characteristics that indicate movement toward this delivery system transition 21st century configuration are key indicators of progress into the future. The continuum of care represents a significant change from the past in permitting patients as consumers to access care that they need and to receive guidance in managing their care with the continuum. All of the partners in the system must recognize their interdependence in the delivery of services and communication of patient activity. When there are breakdowns in the system, it is incumbent on the system to seek to remedy the disruption and to restore the services or connections. Training patients is a mutual responsibility within this environment as the ability of patients to use the services is critically important to curbing costs and improving outcomes. Quality of care and outcomes will be monitored by payers and potential contracting agencies as they determine whether they will participate in the system.

4.3.3 Information System Transition: Isolation to Network

The third process transition is the information system transition. The 20th century column is designated as "information system isolation." The 21st century column is "information system network." This transition maps progress of healthcare organizations along the continuum from isolated computers performing limited tasks to electronic information networks in which employees anywhere in the organization have access to clinical and system information in real time. Identifying characteristics in your organization that align with isolated task-specific computers or information networks and describing them in the appropriate column provide the basis for assessing the progress that your organization is making as it moves from the 20th century model to the 21st century model of healthcare.

The slow journey of electronic information systems in healthcare is the movement from minimal computerization and limited connectivity between task-specific computers to information systems that link all aspects of the healthcare system with clinical and organizational information widely available and with decision support and analytics capabilities. The transition from isolation to networks is the story of the transition from 20th century healthcare to 21st century healthcare. The expansion of networks of electronic information systems with data analysis on a massive scale led to the introduction of industrial quality into healthcare in the late 20th century as the variation and the cost of the care were identified.

For healthcare organizations to advance into the 21st century, it is important that employees have access to information about the way the organization is operating as a whole in real time as well as the actual information required to perform their own work. System knowledge speaks to the accessibility within a healthcare organization of information about the organization itself. In the 20th century, the financial areas were able to gather and analyze large quantities of information to support decision making and for organization planning primarily for senior leadership. In the 21st century, information about the organization needs to be readily available and accessible for employees to be able to evaluate the actual pace of work and resources available to accommodate the needs of the patients and to respond to interruptions in services.

The information system transition assessment chart (Figure 4.7) provides leaders with a way to assess the transition within their organizations from the 20th century information system isolation to the 21st century information system network. The characteristics for each of these models are

20th Century Information System Isolation Characteristics	Points (neg.)	21st Century Information System Network Characteristics	Points (pos.)
Information systems isolated to departments and specific users		Information systems networked throughout the organization	
System data about hospital operations inaccessible outside specific departments		System data about hospital operations accessible wherever needed	
Total (record on scorecard)		Total (record on scorecard)	

Figure 4.7 Information system transition assessment chart.

presented as examples, but the characteristics and number of characteristics will differ by organizations. The characteristics identified with the 20th century information system isolation identify computers and processes within the organization that operate in isolation. This would be computers limited in their scope, disconnected from a broader system and often offering only minimal information to assist in actual patient care. The characteristics associated with the 21st century information system network identify the way computers within the organization form a network that makes communication and data available for clinical support systems and organizational networks for all employees. As these systems expand within organizations they create not only new work flows but also new ways in which individuals and groups share real-time information that affects care and informs decisions and promotes rapid response. As organizations assess their progress from the characteristics of the isolated computers to the characteristics of the network, the organization demonstrates progress along the continuum from the 20th century to the 21st century.

For 20th century healthcare, the handwritten paper medical record remained the central repository of information about the clinical care of patients throughout most of the century. Physicians, nurses and other departments documented information in the medical record and this handwritten record shaped the work flows of staff, limited access to clinical information and sustained the superiority of the physicians in the care of patients by requiring anyone needing clinical information to interpret the handwriting of the physician in the paper medical record.

When computers appeared and were introduced into healthcare, they were used in isolation in specific areas to perform tasks. The areas of the hospital in which data needs required processing large amounts of relatively simple data, such as finance, laboratory, radiology and registration, were areas in which computers first appeared. In the 20th century, data processing remained relatively simple and limited. The results from the computers were often printed and carried by hand to the clinical unit to incorporate them into the medical record. The computer systems of the time were limited in their capability and were difficult to access, and use and the data they generated were often difficult to interpret.

The paper medical record remained foundational to the delivery of care in hospitals throughout the 20th century. The attachment to the paper medical record was hardwired into the work flow and the consciousness of the physicians and other professionals as they delivered care to the patients. As electronic information systems became more sophisticated and capable of replacing the medical record, the process for changing work flows and using the computerized documentation rather than handwritten orders and notes required significant investments of time and staff. This process exemplified the difficulties that healthcare professionals have with change that interrupts processes that are repeated over and over again every day such as documenting patient care and writing orders. It is an accomplishment of 21st century healthcare that the reticence to let go of the paper record was finally overcome as need for access to information transcended the traditions and electronic information systems made the computer record truly useful in the care of the patient.

In the 21st century, the transformative benefits of connectivity and the ability to access and share information to healthcare are recognized and utilized. The technology that creates the networks by establishing a single database for the organization or by linking multiple databases into a whole is the starting point. It is not an easy task to link the data to the professionals and to the patient and have it all come together at the right time and right place to support the right care. The greater challenge for healthcare in moving from the 20th century paper record to the 21st century network is the culture of American healthcare that was born in the handwritten, hardcopy medical record.

Even the documentation in the electronic medical records continues to be patterned after the paper record.

Networks offer the opportunity to create a new image of the medical record into a fluid, flowing, pervasive source of insight in order to remove the ghost of the old medical record from the machine and to build the future. Creating networks that bring multiple databases and systems to the point of care, the data are easily accessible wherever needed and are presented in a form that is easily understandable by the professionals but also, on a certain level, by the patients. The data speak to the care of the patient and help to guide the decision making with support capabilities that translate the various aspects of care into a unified plan that guides the team and informs the patients' decisions.

The walls of the hospital and distance to the patient are no longer impediments to the flow of the information within the network. Essentially, time and space and multiple systems merge into a process that is open to the patient and the care providers and the organizations. This network of information and services creates the healthcare system that is capable of delivering to the patients the right care in the right place at the right time to achieve the right goals and at a cost that is sustainable. It finds its full fruition in the 21st century information system network.

The transition from 20th century isolation to the 21st century network represents the transformation of healthcare from the individual physician in an independent practice to a network that brings teams of professionals together with common access to a large number of clinical databases with evidence-based decision support and real-time monitoring to enable them to respond effectively to the needs of patients at the point of care. This transformation captures an essential element of the movement of American healthcare from the machine to the complex adaptive system. It is the information system transition that makes the creation of the healthcare network a reality.

4.3.4 Financial Transition: Fee-for-Service Financing to Consumer Health Financing

The fourth and final process transition is the financial transition. The 20th century column is designated as "fee-for-service." The 21st century column is "consumer health financing." This transition maps the progress of healthcare organizations as they move from fee-for-service financing to consumer health financing in which patients as consumers reenter the healthcare marketplace. Identifying characteristics in your organization that align with fee-for-service or consumer health financing and describing them in the appropriate column provide the basis for assessing the progress that your organization is making as it moves from the 20th century model to the 21st century model of healthcare.

Initially, payment for healthcare services was either personal payment by the patient to the physician or philanthropic payment by wealthy patrons to charity hospitals to provide charity care to the indigent. With the introduction of technology in the form of operating rooms, laboratories, radiology and professional nurses, physicians persuaded their paying patients to come to the hospital to take advantage of these new technological innovations. Hospitals provided services to meet the requirements of wealthy and middle-class patients and charged for the services. The patient paid a fee for the services.

With the evolution of insurance as the dominant payment process in the 20th century, insurers took premiums primarily from employers, or taxes in the case of Medicare, and used these funds to pay the providers for specific services with rates determined through negotiation. The fee-for-service process was based on patient care orders generated by individual physicians and delivered through a variety of public and private service providers.

In the 21st century, payment for services is moving away from fee-for-service paid by insurers to a system of financing in which the overall services designed to care for patients' health are financed through a combination of payment and risk arrangements involving health systems, insurers, vendors and patients; patients as consumers accept more responsibility for the costs of care and have a greater role in decision making about care and more transparency in the actual costs of care. Health systems, insurers and vendors develop payment processes that involve sharing the risk of financial loss or gain and greater emphasis on the appropriate management of services and outcomes. As healthcare organizations become more sophisticated about their costs and care processes, they will take on more risk of potential financial loss or gain because of confidence they can deliver care for less cost by controlling or removing redundancy and waste. At the same time, consumers are looking for ways to obtain services for less cost and by not depending on the insurers to pay for all services. Progression on the financial continuum involves transparency of costs for services, risk contracting and population health contracting as characteristics consistent with 21st century healthcare.

The financial transition chart (Figure 4.8) is a way for leaders to assess the transition within their organizations from the 20th century fee-for-service payment arrangements to 21st century consumer health financing. The characteristics for each of these models are presented as examples, but the characteristics and number of characteristics will differ depending on the complexity of the design of the organization. As organizations assess their progress from the characteristics of the fee-for-service model to the characteristics of consumer health financing, the organization demonstrates progress along the continuum toward the 21st century.

When all else fails, turn to the consumer to solve the problem. It is in the area of the financial transition that the cost of healthcare comes to represent the shift from 20th century to 21st century healthcare. It is in this area that the difference between the two models is dramatically presented in the transformation of patients into consumers as the last best hope

20th Century Fee-for-Service Characteristics	Points (neg.)	21st Century Consumer Health Financing Characteristics	Points (pos.)
Traditional insurance payment plans		Patients responsible for first dollars	
Insurance pays claims without regard for frequency		Information available on past testing to prevent unnecessary duplication	
Total (record on scorecard)		Total (record on scorecard)	

Figure 4.8 Financial transition chart.

for reducing the costs that were essentially uncontrollable by the vested interests of healthcare in the 20th century. In turning to the consumer of healthcare to control costs, the healthcare industry is admitting its own failures and is setting itself up to compete as any other business. This is quite an admission for an industry that prided itself on being unique and essentially above the dynamics of the marketplace. Though it took trillions of dollars in cost to convince it, American healthcare eventually cried "Uncle" and turned to its own patients, now denoted as "consumers," to bring market discipline to bear on rising costs.

Throughout the 20th century, the patient was either the direct consumer and could access hospital and physician care only with personal payment or the patient was insured and had no real role to play in the payment of services. In the original scenario of personal payment, the physician was the private business person and the patient was a customer. Healthcare operated like the carpenter shop or the grocery store. In the second scenario, the patient was the innocent bystander whose employer took over the role of procuring and managing healthcare in order to keep workers at a time when workers were in short supply. As this model became the dominant model of the 20th century, the insurer and the employer worked with the providers to create a payment system that seemed to work for them without involving the patient. Hidden in the black box of healthcare finances, chargemasters developed out of thin air and payment systems that had nothing to do with quality or outcomes proliferated in an age when technology was the symbol of quality and money for healthcare seemed plentiful.

In the 20th century fee-for-service model, healthcare delivers the service and a fee is paid as in any other transaction in which goods and services are bought and sold. For 20th century healthcare organizations this is the primary method for the exchange. Within this exchange, there are multiple layers of negotiations between providers and payers of all sorts, but the basic model is payment for a specific service or a specific type of care. As insurance and the government replaced the individual patient as the payer, physicians recognized the value of technology to give them better information and the providers realized that the physicians wanted more advanced technology. With the insurers willing to pay the costs for the services ordered by the physicians, the latter part of the 20th century experienced a healthcare "arms race" in which providers sought out ever better equipment and facilities and physicians requested the latest technology. Whatever the physician ordered that was considered reasonable was viewed by the insurers as a service to be paid without concern for the outcomes or frequency of the services. The payer and the hospital negotiated the rates for services and the fees were paid as the services were rendered. Physicians ordered more and the payment process of insurers and hospitals accommodated the increases by raising premiums to the employers and to the federal government. There really was no limit except the ability of employers and payers to pay premiums. In the late 20th century, the costs reached a point at which the entire system could no longer tolerate the increases and the payers changed the rules to focus on quality and outcomes as a way to control costs.

The characteristics associated with the 21st century consumer health financing category point to a very different environment in which the employers and commercial insurers are encouraging patients to become more active in the purchase of healthcare services by increasing their financial participation in the care they receive and designing programs to increase the risk to providers for the quality and costs. From the commercial side, the structure of health insurance is changing due to the yearly increases in costs for health insurance to employers and their employees. These increases were absorbed by the employers in the past, but the increases are now being passed on to employees in the form of much higher deductibles and copays totaling thousands of dollars as the way to keep the premiums lower. In this system, patients are the first payers. Though this approach offers a way to keep the premiums lower for businesses, it significantly increases the costs of healthcare to patients. As a result, patients are once again taking on the role of active consumers of healthcare and acting as customers in their negotiations with providers over costs and quality.

At the same time, through the Medicare program, the federal government is encouraging providers to take responsibility for the health of groups of Medicare patients as a way to reduce costs by eliminating unnecessary services while improving the health of patients by ensuring that appropriate services are received. Medicare is reducing payments to providers under the Affordable Care Act and encouraging the providers to enter into agreements with Medicare to be accountable for the care of groups of patients that are affiliated with their organizations through their owned-physician practices. In these accountable care organizations, the hospitals or physicians agree to meet certain quality measures and to work to reduce costs through better management of patient care. In exchange for more active management of care of Medicare patients, the providers have the opportunity to receive a portion of the savings achieved by reductions in the use of services, which results from better management of care.

The shift from the insurance fee-for-service coverage of the 20th century to the consumer health financing of the 21st century requires significant changes in the way consumers behave and in the way that providers behave in the marketplace of healthcare. For the consumers who are thrust back into the marketplace in a sudden fashion as employer insurance programs place high upfront costs on them, the initial response is shock and then they begin to act as customers. No longer protected by insurance, healthcare customers are looking for ways to reduce costs while ensuring that they obtain the care that they need to protect their health.

In this new environment, customer expectations of healthcare providers change significantly. They expect the providers they are now paying directly for healthcare services to treat them as customers in the same way that those other service providers treat them. Many other service providers used industrial quality techniques to redesign processes to be more efficient and more convenient for their customers. Healthcare, on the other hand, has only marginally embraced industrialization and effective network information systems and is unprepared in terms of Lean and Six Sigma techniques to meet the expectations of their newly created customers. Healthcare providers are still focused on the physician as the de facto customer, the insurer as the payer and the patient as the compliant material that they process.

The physicians are as unprepared as the hospitals and other providers to respond to the needs of patients as customers in the new healthcare marketplace. As physicians order services in the traditional way and refer to the hospitals, their patients as customers are asking about the costs of care and whether the tests or procedures are necessary. They are asking their physicians for alternatives to the hospital that may be cheaper but still provide quality care. The physicians in most cases are not prepared for these questions and are frustrated at suddenly being thrust into the role of advising patients on alternatives. In this environment, many patients are making decisions and seeking out other sources of information in addition to physicians. They are rejecting physician recommendations in many cases and seeking out alternatives. Pharmacists, urgent care locations, walk-in clinics, and online chat groups are all becoming sources of healthcare information that are less expensive and more easily accessible than physicians.

Hospitals as the primary source of healthcare services during the 20th century fee-for-service environment are finding their role in the new healthcare marketplace to be challenging as patients seek more information about and alternatives to the high costs of hospitalization. Information concerning the costs of care is the most obvious area in which hospitals are struggling to respond to the new customer status of patients. As physicians order tests and surgical procedures, patients are contacting the hospital to find out the cost and what they will need to pay. Hospitals are often unable to manage these questions because the information is simply not available in many cases. Care processes and their associated costs are not well defined. With only marginal implementation of Lean and Six Sigma, hospitals have not clearly identified the costs associated with care. They have also not defined the processes related to specific diagnoses sufficiently to be able to present the potential costs to the patients. Due to the physicians and hospitals using separate billing processes, hospitals are not prepared to offer a final cost figure that includes all services and providers. For customers who are conditioned to much more efficient systems of pricing and billing, healthcare seems frustratingly unable to offer even minimal assistance to customers.

From the Medicare and commercial insurance side of 21st century consumer health financing, providers and physicians are encouraged to take on more responsibility for overall management of the care of patients. Insurers and the government hold providers of care responsible for quality measures designed to preserve the health of their patients in order to prevent them from overuse of expensive hospital services. This new accountability requires physician practices to bring their chronically ill patients into the office for examinations and to refer them for more frequent testing as a way to reduce the potential for Emergency Department admissions to the hospital. Care coordinators oversee these care processes and are often the contacts between the patients and the physicians. Since patients are the first payers for services, these requests for trips to the physician's office or for testing require the patient to pay for the additional services.

For providers such as hospitals, Medicare views the entire episode of care as the basis for determining whether costs have been reduced through better management of care. This means that hospitals and physician groups that participate in accountable care are at risk for care delivered after the patient leaves the hospital. In order to manage post-acute care, which accounts for a significant portion of Medicare costs, hospitals are creating new relationships with skilled nursing facilities and with home health agencies to work to reduce costs while preventing patients from readmission into the hospital.

In addition to the accountable care programs, which address overall costs, Medicare has implemented programs that penalize hospitals that experience readmissions, mortalities or complications at rates that are considered excessive for patients with diagnoses that are frequently admitted to the hospital. Again, for hospitals that have only recently begun the process of industrialization and have only marginally embraced the techniques for improving processes, these programs represent the potential for significant monetary losses due to the quality of care as well as Medicare's methods of data collection.

For consumers, healthcare is a service like other services and in the 21st century this means that all aspects of the service delivery process must be designed to meet the needs of patients who have choices and who are encouraged to seek lower cost alternatives. Healthcare is notorious for its inability to help patients understand what they are buying and what it costs. In the current environment, many healthcare organizations are not able to provide information on the full scope of possible costs associated with procedures and tests. They are also not able to provide cost information that indicates what the patient is at risk to pay prior to procedures and tests. The lack of consumer information on the full scope of procedures and tests and the actual costs is one of the clearest indications that many healthcare organizations are not prepared to support consumer health financing in the 21st century.

Without full disclosure about the scope of tests and procedures or the costs, patients are not able to use the normal market dynamics to search out lower cost options that may reduce their costs and encourage other providers to lower costs. The power of the patient as a consumer to bring healthcare costs and quality back into an acceptable range requires the same transparency as other services in the marketplace. Inviting patients as consumers into the healthcare marketplace means more than just changing the financing processes. It means recognizing that consumers today are more knowledgeable about healthcare and have been conditioned by other industries that took the Lean and Six Sigma path to expect a high level of service that is commensurate with the price. As a consumer product, then, the presentation of the healthcare services and the expectations of the consumers become much more important. Most healthcare situations in which consumers would seek services require a number of different services and these can be delivered by various agencies. Healthcare in most cases is not able to provide patients with packages of services that are bundled together for specific diagnoses and to offer specific pricing. Rather, healthcare has created a pricing process in which the physician is a craftsman and every patient is expected to pay what he or she would pay a craftsman for highly customized services.

Rethinking the design and packaging of healthcare services is a critically important aspect of the pricing that is required for healthcare organizations to succeed in the 21st century. The design of the products must address the connections that consumers make between various services rather than simply the clinical perspective of providers. Access to multiple ways to receive services improves the convenience, which can be important in making consumer decisions. The packaging of healthcare services requires clear explanations of what is provided and what the cost will be. The benefits that consumers can expect are important to the purchase process and price, but healthcare organizations struggle to decide what benefit can be expected from their services. To do this, healthcare providers and insurers need to design new ways of communicating to consumers about their services that go beyond the negotiations over price. They also need to know the expected outcomes and the guarantees included in the purchase and the other value expectations such as accessibility, convenience and responsiveness. These new demands on providers and insurers require American healthcare to finally become accountable to the patient as a consumer who actually has a financial stake in his or her healthcare and is comparing healthcare to other services.

Ultimately, as consumers take a more active role in the future in shopping for healthcare services, the providers will need to develop new ways to help consumers in the same way that other companies support consumers in the marketplace. Outcomes and guarantees became important as consumers want information on what they are actually purchasing, how it will be delivered and what they should expect. For the first time, providers have to take the outcomes of care as described by the consumers of care as important to their business. Patient surveys and focus groups take on new importance as service providers seek to understand how these new consumers make decisions and how they choose where to go for care. New delivery processes shaped by consumer preferences such as walk-in clinics and urgent care offices may begin to replace the traditional office practice and hospital stay. As healthcare organizations implement industrial quality and begin to move from fee-for-service to consumer health financing, engagement with patients as consumers and decision makers will transform the exchange process and will challenge healthcare in new ways to respond to the 21st century healthcare environment.

4.4 Cultural Transitions

Of all the transitions, the cultural transitions represent perhaps the most difficult because they are at the heart of American healthcare's conception of itself. Born out of the 19th century and refined throughout the 20th century, these transitions reflect fundamental aspects of healthcare that are going through profound changes in the 21st century. There are iconic images that reflect profound truths of the 20th century. There are not, however, clearly defined images that are associated with 21st century healthcare. This makes the transition between the 20th and 21st century all the more difficult to grasp because there is no clear sense of the need to change these cultural elements. To move into the future, however, these transitions must occur.

The professional transition describes the professionalization of the physician that occurred in the 19th and early 20th centuries and shaped the role of physicians and the operations of hospitals in the early stages of their development. As healthcare coalesced around the physician and hospital during the 20th century, the physicians—through the structure of the medical staff in the local hospital and the national lobbying of the American Medical Association—had a profound effect on healthcare. This professionalization and the efforts of the AMA supported the image of the physician as a craftsman with unique skills who directed the care of patients with autonomy. There was no one else in healthcare that possessed the skills or the knowledge of the physician and this gave the physician a singular role in making all of the decisions related to the care of patients. In moving into the 21st century, the physician's role as an autonomous professional with unique privileges becomes an obstacle to the efficiency of the health system and to the work of multiple disciplines in the delivery of care. The industrialization of healthcare challenges the 20th century image of the physician's autonomy and pushes for an integrated team in which the physicians function as leaders—but leaders in the 21st century sense of supporting the team in achieving patient goals rather than as the unique status of arbiter of all decisions.

The metaphor transition operates on many levels in healthcare organizations, but the subtlety of a metaphor within the context of an organization makes it difficult to recognize the importance. For many people, the question of whether healthcare should be viewed as a machine or as a complex adaptive system makes little difference in their daily work. However, the reality of this metaphorical shift is truly profound when it is recognized that the image of the organization as held in the minds and imaginations of leaders and employees serves as a guide and motivational force that shapes decisions and operations of the organization. The importance of this transitional shift is echoed on a lower level by all the transitions. This transition, however, speaks to the overall perspective we hold of our organizations and healthcare and describes the overall shift that other transitions support. This metaphorical transition guides the other transitions and is realized as the other transitions progress toward the 21st century model.

4.4.1 Professional Transition: Autonomy to Integration

The first of the cultural transitions is the professional transition. The 20th century column is designated as "professional autonomy." The 21st century column is "professional integration." The focus of this transition is the progress of healthcare organizations as they move along the continuum from the autonomous healthcare professionals to the integration of healthcare professionals into the team structure of the 21st century industrialized organization. Identifying characteristics in your organization that align with professional autonomy or to professional integration and describing them in the appropriate column provide the basis for assessing the progress that your organization is making as it moves from the 20th century model to the 21st century model of healthcare.

The growth of physician professionalism in the late 19th and early 20th centuries was a significant factor in shaping American medicine because it created the basis for the autonomy of the physician. The autonomy of the physician established the clinical structure and decision-making processes in American medicine and healthcare. Decisions affecting patient care ultimately resided with the orders of the physician. Requirements for university education, state licensure and medical staff membership in hospitals further supported this structure. This professional autonomy also separated the physician from the bureaucracy of the hospital and led to the creation of a parallel system based on democratic processes within the organization of the medical staff and outside the structures of hospital operations.

In the 21st century, the autonomy and prerogatives of physicians are slowly changing as multidisciplinary teams of care providers bring new knowledge and skills to the care process. The centralization of clinical care in the physician has been eroded by the availability of clinical information to broad groups of care providers and has moved to a view of healthcare that is focused on the patient rather than the physician. This is a more integrated care process in which physicians are team members rather than sole providers and care decisions are based on the expertise needed to meet the patients' goals.

20th Century Professional Autonomy Characteristics	Points (neg.)	21st Century Professional Integration Characteristics	Points (pos.)
Professional autonomy practiced		Integrated teams of professionals including physicians	
Social deference practiced toward certain professions		Social deference explicitly excluded from integrated teams	
Total (record on scorecard)		Total (record on scorecard)	

Figure 4.9   Professional transition assessment chart.

The professional transition assessment chart (Figure 4.9) offers leaders a way to assess the transition within their organizations from the 20th century professional autonomy to the 21st century professional integration. The characteristics for each of these models are presented as examples, but the characteristics and number of characteristics will differ depending on the complexity of the design of the organization. As organizations assess their progress from the characteristics of professional autonomy to the characteristics of professional integration, the organization demonstrates progress along the continuum toward the 21st century.

The characteristics identified with the 20th century professional autonomy reflect the profound effect of physician autonomy resulting from the professionalization that occurred in the 19th and 20th centuries and continues today. The professional status of the physician affected all aspects of healthcare throughout the 20th century. Through a variety of legal and regulatory measures as well as the cultural promotion by the American Medical Association and the local hospital medical staff, the physician truly stands as a singularly powerful shaping force. This force shapes not only the work flows of healthcare organizations that require physician orders and authorization, but also the deliberation of nonclinical issues within organizations. Due to the status of physicians often emphasized by long white lab coats, discussions in meetings and decisions on issues that are unrelated to medical expertise often hinge on the personal preference of physicians. Their role has been regarded as unique even among professionals, and physicians have developed a singular professional stature characterized by autonomy in their decision making concerning patients from any nonpeers in the practice of medicine.

The structure and operation of the 20th century healthcare organization modeled the scientific management of the industrial age in its bureaucracy, but the professional affiliation of the medical staff remained outside this structure. The professional side of healthcare organizations often maintained its separateness in relation to the rest of the organization and used this separateness to structure activities and work as a separate entity within the hospital.

The deference to the physician goes even further in hospital operations that are shaped by the decisions of physicians. In this world, visual cues such as long white coats of the scientist or expert signified individuals designated as decision makers and authorized to direct the work of others and to require obedience from others. Accountable only to their peers, physicians shaped the processes of care to meet their needs and used the clinical staff as personal support staff. The decisions of the physician were not to be questioned since only another physician was capable of questioning the decisions of physicians. Social deference to the status of the physician was expected and supported through training and orientation of other staff. The professional autonomy of the physician rested on the structure of society and on organizations that promoted the idea that the physician and the physician alone was capable of directing the vast armamentarium used to cure patients and heal injuries. Anything that supported the physician benefitted the patient.

In the 21st century professional integration view, the separateness of the physician as an autonomous professional in healthcare organizations fades and in its place is the integration of the physician into a multidisciplinary team in which many disciplines have a voice in the care of patients and the patients are viewed as under the care of the organization and team rather than a single professional. The physician's professional status is viewed from the functional perspective as it serves to facilitate the work of the team of professionals caring for the patients. It is not permitted to outweigh other factors or to restrict the contributions of other team members. As members of the healthcare multidisciplinary team, physicians participate along with other disciplines in the deliberations of the team, and the skills and knowledge of all the members of the team are given a place in the discussion. The physician is no longer viewed as an autonomous decision maker, but rather as one voice, albeit an important voice, in the decisions of the team.

The 21st century model reflects the complexity of patient care in all its dimensions and the importance of addressing this complexity with a full complement of skills, experience and talent. This new approach requires a team with members from a number of disciplines able to work effectively together and with the patients. Because of the complexity of patient needs and the speed necessary to develop a plan and to execute it, disciplines come together with the patient to identify goals, develop plans and produce the necessary results quickly. Through industrialization, organizations transitioning toward the 21st century identify the many elements of 20th century healthcare culture and processes that emphasized the dominance and autonomy of the physician as counterproductive and working against the effectiveness of the integration of the disciplines into a cohesive group. The role of the physician remains very strong within the clinical dimensions due to the structures of licensure, medical staff privileging and other societal and legal aspects of patient care. However, the vestiges of preferential treatment such as special attire, autonomous decision making, peer accountability outside the team and social deference are significantly reduced if not eliminated. In place of these structures that supported the professional autonomy of the physician is patient-focused team decision making and accountability.

With the introduction of industrialized healthcare and the emergence of 21st century healthcare, the illusion of the lone physician battling illness and injury as a personal crusade gave way to the search for value as defined by the patients. Focusing on the patient requires a team of disciplines because of the complexity of the patient's situation and the redefinition of value as what the patient is seeking from care. In this new environment, the members of the team are the armamentarium of healthcare and their expertise and willingness to work with other disciplines is critical to the success of the care process.

The integration of a spectrum of disciplines into a team requires a parity that permits the free exchange of ideas and views and the willingness to speak out if something is not working. Visual cues signifying status become a distraction to the free exchange of information and views. Accountability is to the team in the fulfillment of the needs of the patient. This accountability requires physicians as well as other disciplines to see themselves as members of the group and accountable to the group. Decisions are developed as a group in which the patient plays a major role and each of the disciplines contributes. Finally, the social deference toward the physician is the past and offers no benefit to the team. The focus is on the patient rather than the preferences of an individual on the team.

4.4.2 Metaphor Transition: Scientific Machine to Complex Adaptive System

The second cultural transition is the metaphor transition. The 20th century column is designated as "scientific machine." The 21st century column is "complex adaptive system." The focus of this transition is the progress of healthcare organizations as they move along the continuum from the scientific machine image of the organization to a complex adaptive system view. Identifying characteristics in your organization that align with the mechanistic perspective or to the complex adaptive system in the appropriate column provides the basis for assessing the progress that your organization is making as it moves from the 20th century model to the 21st century model of healthcare.

A metaphor is the application of a concept or image to an unrelated concept or image to create new understanding. Metaphors are the way we understand the world—not just a figure of speech. Metaphors applied to healthcare shape our understanding of healthcare. Metaphors applied to organizations direct what we improve, how we improve and the goals we set for improvement. Metaphors are often invisible to us. Like the "light bulb of an idea" or the "leg of a table" they are part of our thoughts and speech, but we fail to see how they shape our understanding (Morgan 1993, 2006; Lakoff and Johnson 1980).

Two competing healthcare organizational metaphors appear frequently in the literature about 20th century and 21st century healthcare: the scientific machine metaphor and the complex adaptive system metaphor. The scientific machine metaphor is based on the Newtonian view of identified causes and predictable effects and well-ordered organizational structures amenable to planning and control. This concept is expressed organizationally as specific actions leading to specific results to meet management's defined goals. In healthcare, the 20th century model of the hospital as similar to a factory striving for efficiency with a bureaucratic departmental structure and a leadership structure based on hierarchical management in which centralized leadership designs the work expresses this scientific and mechanistic metaphor view.

The metaphor of the complex adaptive system actually merges three organizational metaphors into one phrase. Complexity addresses the many parts of healthcare organizations that are linked together through information systems. The adaptive aspect of healthcare reflects the need for healthcare to respond to changes in its environment. As communities, regulations, technology and demographics of populations change, healthcare organizations must adapt to the changes in order to maintain their fit within the overall environment within which they function in order to meet the needs of the customer they serve. Finally, healthcare as a system reflects the way in which the mission and vision and values tie the individuals and groups within the organization together by a common purpose. The fundamental statements of beliefs and the simple rules that reflect these beliefs and structure operations are expressed thousands of times each day in the activities of everyone who works in the organization (Wheatley 1992; Zimmerman et al. 2001; Morgan 1993, 2006; Uhl-Bien and McKelvey 2008; Crowell 2011).

The metaphor transition assessment chart (Figure 4.10) offers a means for leaders to evaluate the progress within their organizations from the 20th century scientific machine to the 21st century complex adaptive system. The organizational characteristics for each of these metaphors are presented as examples, but the characteristics and number of characteristics will differ depending on the complexity and design of the organization. The characteristics identified with the 20th century scientific machine metaphor reflect the 20th century application of scientific management to the mechanistic structure of the bureaucracy with the goal of achieving the same high level of efficiency that was produced in industry. By using the image as the metaphor for the organization, hospitals in the early 20th century sought to create a scientific

20th Century Scientific Machine Characteristics	Points (neg.)	21st Century Complex Adaptive System Characteristics	Points (pos.)
Machine descriptions commonly used to describe organizational operations		Complex adaptive system descriptions commonly used to describe organizational operations	
Clearly defined bureaucracy		Complex systems recognized as structure of the organization	
Total (record on scorecard)		Total (record on scorecard)	

Figure 4.10 Metaphor transition assessment chart.

image that would instill confidence in physicians and prospective patients and encourage them to use the hospital. This also fit well with the introduction of technology into the hospital as the basis for high-quality healthcare services and the use of accounting to evaluate costs and revenues.

The characteristics associated with the 21st century complex adaptive system bring to light a very different organizational culture and environment than the one that bred the scientific machine. The complex adaptive system world of 21st century healthcare looks to new images that more accurately reflect the complexity, adaptability and system structure of modern healthcare organizations. Through the use of information systems to create networks and the resulting availability of information, new structures appear spontaneously as individuals and groups react to changes and the organizations continuously adapt at the point of interface with the environment. As organizations assess their progress from the characteristics of the scientific machine model to the characteristics of complex adaptive system, the organization demonstrates progress along the continuum toward the 21st century.

In the 19th century in America, healthcare for the middle and upper classes was delivered in the home by a physician in large cities or by an experienced healer in villages. There was a sense in which healthcare was a family concern, with assistance provided from outside the family only in cases of serious illness. The home as the setting for healthcare and the family as the healthcare providers made up the basic structure of care for the sick or injured until the last century.

As healthcare moved out of the home and family setting and into the hospital to take advantage of the scientific discoveries associated with aseptic surgery, x-rays and laboratories, a new structure began to emerge for the nascent healthcare organization to bring scientific management to healthcare. This structure actually developed in industry, particularly in manufacturing and railroads, before it migrated to healthcare. The idea was that a factory or a hospital was an organization in which different parts work together the way a machine operates and with the same efficiency. Leadership at the top of the organization sends messages to the managers and the managers direct the workers. The work of the individual workers is carefully designed to be efficient and to fit the operation of the organization. With machine-like efficiency, each worker performs the work and the managers ensure that the work is performed correctly and communicate the results to the leaders. The image of organizations as efficient machines remained the dominant metaphor and the aspiration of leaders throughout the late 19th century and the 20th century. Hospitals, like other organizations, were to operate efficiently under the control of the superintendent or the administrator and the bureaucracy.

The 20th century hospital was born at the time when scientific management and the machine metaphor were in ascendancy. In the flush of the second industrial revolution and at a time in healthcare when science was opening up all the secrets to life and prosperity, creating a well-designed bureaucracy in the hospital and operating it as an efficient machine seemed to be the path to delivering a new quality of life in America. As management embraced this new approach as more effective than the view of healthcare as a family enterprise, organizational charts with clearly defined leadership and departments and lines of accountability appeared as diagrams for the organizational machines. Employees were given specific instruction on their work and their managers were held accountable for the work and for reporting to the leadership. Accounting and operational information was provided to the central leadership to guide future decisions on the areas that were not meeting expectations. Fine-tuning the operation by issuing directives to managers reinforced the role of the central leadership controlling the organization.

This model for the operational side of healthcare continued into the 21st century with only minimal changes. Administrators and managers were trained to follow it with an occasional nod to the role of employees in the success of the organization. The impetus to sustain and expand the machine metaphor came with industrialization of healthcare as the medical staff was incorporated into the operations side of the hospital as payers demanded improved processes and outcomes like those in other industries. New information systems provided more data on operations and output and provided better tools for control. Expectations for predictable results expanded as well from payers tired of seeing cost increases with little to show for the expenses.

This image was applied during this period to the operation of the hospital, but not to the work of the medical staff. The hospital and the medical staff coexisted essentially in the same building but operated in very different ways. Since the medical staff was not under the direct control of the management staff in the hospital, the doctors were not required to place efficiency as their highest priority. In fact, the medical staff functioned as craftsmen or artisans within the machine of the hospital and disrupted the pursuit of efficiency that administrators professed to value the most. This is the inherent paradox of American healthcare that ultimately led to the inefficiencies of the late 20th century.

As the public and government became aware of cost, errors and other inefficiencies occurring within healthcare, the final mechanical solution, the completion of the machine metaphor, appeared as the industrialization of healthcare in the early 21st century. The industrialization of healthcare broadened the metaphor of the machine beyond the operational bureaucracy of the hospital that had always aspired to operational efficiency to now include the medical staff in the hospital. This new industrialization required that the product of the hospital—namely, the actual processes and outcomes of care—be efficient and produce quality commensurate with its costs. The medical staff, for the first time in the history of American medicine, was to be held accountable for the cost and quality of hospital production based on the same statistical process controls and outcome data that manufacturing used to measure efficiency and quality of production.

In the 21st century healthcare complex adaptive system model, the focus is on the results of the new initiative of industrialization. Through the industrialization of healthcare organizations, the entirety of healthcare organizations is brought within the dominant metaphor of the machine. Surprisingly, the new metaphor of the complex adaptive system emerged spontaneously from the implementation of this industrialization as healthcare information technology and networks were established within healthcare. In place of the paper medical record, hospitals began to implement electronic medical records and to expand organizational information networks that connected large numbers of employees throughout each healthcare organization. Communication and information became available in real time to large numbers of people throughout the organization. Systems appeared through the links of the networks and changes began to occur in the processes as people shared information. Clinical information was no longer confined to the hardcopy medical record or to an isolated database in a department. No longer were physicians or organization leadership the only ones with access to information. With the advent of these information systems, the clinical processes and the work of the organization's operations were open to the scrutiny and commentary of employees throughout the hospital.

The shift from a mechanistic image to a complex adaptive system perspective is occurring less because of conscious efforts to redesign organizations and more because of the implementation of information systems and the speed at which change is creating the need for adaptive response from within the organization. The new information networks link more and more organizations together and, as information flows between the organizations, they react spontaneously at the operational level and as a result change occurs in unpredictable ways. A new image appears in which multiple individuals and groups are linked together and, through many decisions and responses, every day create the complex adaptive system of the healthcare organization of the future.

Tracking the evolution of the dominant metaphors of the organization provides a way for leadership to assess the transition from the machine or mechanistic image to the image of a complex adaptive system. The dominant metaphors within healthcare organizations frequently appear in the messages that leadership delivers concerning expectations for organizations and methods for achieving goals.

When the scientific machine metaphor is dominant, then the message aligns with the hierarchical chart of the organization and the expectations of leadership require that specific positions or individuals accomplish specific goals using specified resources. The ability to produce specific results by the application of specific resources and the confidence that the predicted results will occur speak to the scientific machine metaphor as supporting the ability of leadership to decide what should be done and the ability of a designated individual to do it. Control and predictability are the hallmarks of machine metaphor.

In organizations in which the complex adaptive system metaphor shapes the thinking of leadership, the focus of leadership shifts dramatically. Recognizing that the central leadership is not the source of knowledge about the organization or its customers, the leaders clearly express the mission and vision and values of the organization to the people and encourage them to discover the best ways to live these beliefs at the interface between the organization and the environment. They model the fundamental beliefs of the organization as they seek out opportunities to learn from the interactions between the organization and its customers and the indications of the success of these interactions. They look for positive signs of success in the innovations occurring at the edge of the organization and seek to learn how to support the spread of these innovations. They seek to learn from groups of customers and groups of employees what is needed to meet their needs and what new services are helpful to patients. Out of these conversations between leadership, the employees and the customer, leadership develops the broad goals that reflect the mission and vision and values and expresses these to the employees. Leadership communicates back to the employees the progress in reaching the goals and asks for guidance in supporting the work and accelerating the learning opportunities.

Relationships take the place of command and control and rapid responses based on conversations take the place of meetings. Flexibility and simple rules guide the processes of the organizations as employees at all levels recognize their ability to identify changes, develop ideas and collaborate with others to make changes. The focus is on the flow of information in the organization as well as between its patients and customers. With each additional piece of information and each interaction, everyone is able to add to the common knowledge of the organization and to work with others to open up new opportunities for better services and increased efficiency and greater success for the patients, the customers and the organization.

Using the complex adaptive system metaphor in place of the scientific machine of the 20th century provides a more meaningful and useful image of the organization for the future. Rather than mechanical control and predictive results, the organization thinks of itself as growing and developing within the environment. It recognizes new opportunities as they appear and incorporates this knowledge into an understanding of itself. There is less emphasis on declaring what it is and what it intends to do and more focus on discovering what it is and what it can do. Ultimately the organization seeks to grow and finds its purpose by discovering the strengths that come from complexity and the freedom that comes from adaptation. In this way it moves beyond the limitations of the machine image and moves to create a greater understanding of its potential beyond the walls of the hospital. Reaching out into the community in seeking its purpose, the hospital of the 21st century absorbs within itself the aspirations of its patients and customers and blends them with the abilities and knowledge of its employees to create a new way to deliver healthcare (Wheatley 1992; Morgan 1993, 2006; Zimmerman et al. 2001; Uhl-Bien and McKelvey 2008; Crowell 2011).

4.5 The Transition Scorecard and Transition Progress Scale

Organizational assessment begins with the individual transition assessment charts for each of the ten transitions. The transition assessment charts consist of columns describing 20th century and 21st century characteristics of organizations and positive and negative columns. For the transitions, the organizational characteristics are assessed and a negative 1 is assigned when the characteristic reflects the 20th century model and a positive 1 is assigned when the characteristic reflects the 21st century model as described in the transition assessment charts. It is recommended that organizations identify five characteristics initially for each transition assessment chart column. The totals of the 20th century and the 21st century from each of the transition assessment charts are transferred to the organizational transition scorecard.

The transition scorecard provides a way to review the point totals for the ten transitions and to develop the final total that can be conveyed to the transition progress scale. The scorecard also provides a comparison of the transitions to identify which are impeding progress the most and which have progressed the farthest. When the final number is transferred to the scale, the overall progress of the organization as reflected in the aggregate of all ten transitions will be displayed for a particular date.

The total from the organizational transition scorecard (Figure 4.11) is transferred to the overall transition progress scale (Figure 4.12). The transition progress scale is the total of the assessments of all ten transitions. The final totals for all the 20th century points and 21st century points are summed to determine the transition progress scale reading for a given date. Transition progress scales can be compared over time to assess overall movement.

Organizations begin at the center or zero on the transition progress scale. A larger negative number moves the organization toward the 20th century end of the scale and represents a lack of progress. A larger positive number moves the organization toward the 21st century and represents progress in adapting to the new healthcare model. A total of fifty points are possible in either direction based on the five characteristics that are identified for each of the ten transitions.

Transition Scorecard	20th Century (neg. no.)	21st Century (pos. no.)	Total (sum neg. and pos.)
Organizational structure: hierarchy to complex system			
Organizational relationship: transactional to emergent			
Leadership: control to trust			
Innovation: centralized to adaptive			
Production method: craftsman to multidisciplinary team			
Delivery system: hospital to continuum of care			
Information system: isolation to network			
Financial: fee-for-service to consumer health financing			
Professional: autonomy to integration			
Metaphor: scientific machine to complex adaptive system			
Totals (transfer sum to transition progress scale)			

Figure 4.11   Organizational transition scorecard.

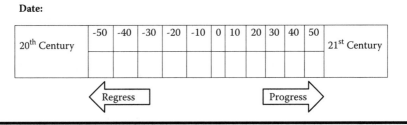

Figure 4.12   Transition progress scale.

Chapter 5

A Vision of 21st Century Healthcare

5.1 Introduction

Industrialized healthcare in the form of Lean and Six Sigma initiatives and expanding information systems pushes organizations out of the 20th century and into the 21st, but it is not the image of the future. The ten transitions for healthcare's journey to the 21st century provide a description of the movement of organizations between the traditions and practices of the 20th century and the anticipated structures and operations of the 21st century. The transition progress scale provides a framework for assessing movement between the past and the future.

As healthcare organizations transition into the future, they need images of the future to serve as guides. These images or generative metaphors provide a sense of common direction that can be understood by employees and a goal that challenges and motivates them to achieve their future. Each of the ten transitions involves a movement from one metaphor to another that coincides with the movement from the 20th century to the 21st century at the overall transition level, as well as at the level of each characteristic within the transitions. For each transition, the heading in the 20th century column is the metaphor or image that describes a key aspect of 20th century healthcare. These images or metaphors for the 20th century are hierarchy, transaction, control, centralized, craftsman, hospital, isolation, fee-for-service, autonomy, and scientific machine.

The generative metaphor is the 21st century image that is the heading for the second column in each transition. The generative metaphors challenge the existing metaphors of the 20th century as no longer sufficient and encourage and guide organizational change toward the future. These metaphors describe the anticipated structures, operations and values of 21st century healthcare organizations and motivate and guide the progress along the continuum within the transitions toward the future. These images or generative metaphors for the 21st century are complex system, emergent, trust, adaptive, multidisciplinary, continuum of care, network, consumer, integration and complex adaptive system.

The overarching metaphor for the 20th century is the scientific machine exemplified in the factory image of the hospital as a healthcare production facility. It embodies the Newtonian view of organizations as efficient, predictable and bureaucratic organizations captured in the deceptively simple organization chart. A geometric image that can be associated with this metaphor is the square. The square figure captures the precision and definition of 20th century views and resembles the foundation of the hospital that is the quintessential depiction of 20th century healthcare.

The overarching metaphor for the 21st century is the complex adaptive system. This metaphor brings together the complexity of individuals and groups that make up organizations into systems that are bound together by common mission, vision and values and the expression of these fundamental beliefs in adapting to rapidly changing internal and external environments in a never-ending process of change, evolution and emergence. Gone are the clear lines and predicable end points. In geometric terms, this metaphor of healthcare in the 21st century is the "circle of care" or the geometric image of a multipointed star. This incorporates the vision of healthcare delivery as a complex adaptive system that is based on the needs of the patient and incorporates all the modalities from self-care to acute care and the informational links that bring them all together.

This chapter presents the future state of healthcare that is beginning to emerge. It appears as progress is made in the transitions that were identified as the implementation of industrialization created the more perfect machine of healthcare that was imagined but only partly realized in the 20th century. In this vision of 21st century healthcare, the patient becomes the focus with less distraction from the mystery of the payment process and less confusion on the role of the physician in determining the value of the care that is provided. In this new future, the system is designed to respond more efficiently and more effectively to the needs and to the goals of the patient as the customer.

The next section, "Generative Metaphors of the 21st Century," offers the guiding visions of the new state of healthcare discovered in the generative metaphors that form the goals of the ten transitions. For leaders and organizations, learning to use the 21st century goals of the transitions as the generative metaphors for 21st century healthcare provides an effective tool for motivating and guiding people and organizations toward the future.

Section 5.3, "The 21st Century Circle of Care," offers an illustration of the type of system that may lie ahead for healthcare and for patients. In the circle of care, patients are able to access a variety of services and service providers while always being recognized and guided by the information systems. The system is designed to deliver care when the patient needs and desires it in ways that reduce costs while maintaining quality. As a circle, an image that contrasts with the square of the 20th century hospital, the end of an episode of care is always the beginning of services designed to support good health and to respond to injury and illness.

5.2 Generative Metaphors of the 21st Century

Metaphors provide understanding by applying insights and characteristics of one image to expand and enlighten the understanding of another image. When generative metaphors (Schön 1979; Barrett and Copperrider 1990) are used, the initial metaphor is the current understanding and the generative metaphor is an image or understanding that challenges the current view. The power of the generative metaphor lies in the creation of a new understanding built on a new image. For American healthcare, the existing metaphor is 20th century healthcare that is reflected in the 20th century column headings in all ten transitions. The generative metaphor is the vision of 21st century healthcare that challenges it and is presented in the 21st century column headings in all ten transitions (Goodwin 2013).

The generative metaphors of 21st century American healthcare use images emerging out of industrialization as it spreads through healthcare. These images challenge the 20th century images by presenting a new, more powerful view of the future. As healthcare progresses along the continuums within each of the ten transitions, the images in the 21st century column become clearer and more persuasive as the images that are relevant. With the movement toward the future, the 20th century column characteristics become less convincing as images of the future and recede into the background as the organization progresses along the continuum toward 21st century healthcare.

The images or concepts in the 21st century column create a different picture or understanding of a fundamental aspect of healthcare than is presented by the metaphors in the 20th century column. These new metaphors challenge the familiar concepts associated with 20th century healthcare and, as people within the organization see greater relevance and meaning in the new metaphors, they use these metaphors in understanding the organization and their work. As they use these new metaphors to design and perform their work, they actually move the organization forward in the continuums toward becoming a 21st century healthcare organization in reality.

In the organizational structure transition, the metaphor of hierarchy represented by the organizational chart is one of the most common metaphors representing the structures and relationships in organizations in the 20th century. Healthcare organizations share this metaphor of the 20th century, which typically consists of boxes and lines representing departments, positions, power and accountability. Based on the scientific management of the 20th century, it is iconic throughout healthcare. So powerful is this metaphor of an organization that the generative metaphor must truly inspire a desire for change if organizations are to progress.

The iconic image of the 21st century that has emerged to challenge the vertical organizational chart is the complex system. Based on the concept of complexity as multiple entities involved in activities and formed into a system by common mission, vision and values, this image promotes a strong view of relationships. This generative metaphor challenges the heart of 20th century organizations by describing the organization in terms of the way that employees actually relate to each other rather than in the arbitrary design of a central authority that consists of positional power structured for bureaucratic power and control. The continued dominance of hierarchical organizational charts demonstrates the strength of the metaphor in healthcare.

The contrasting metaphors in the organizational relationship transition are the transactional relationship and the emergent relationship as descriptions of employment in healthcare organizations. The future of healthcare appears very different from the past in these two metaphors. Transactional relationships between organizations and their employees consisting of specific departments with specific functions and employees with carefully defined work responsibilities are the 20th century metaphor for employment born of 19th century scientific management. The relationships between the employees and the organization are transactional in that each person is viewed as a component of a specific area that performs specific tasks in specific ways. These actions are then tied to other actions performed by other employees in the machinery of the organization. Job descriptions and other defining documents specify the work and the way the work is to be performed. As components or parts of the organization performing specific tasks, transactional employees are given only the information needed to perform their tasks.

Challenging the metaphor of the transactional relationship of the 20th century worker to the organization is a 21st century generative metaphor of the emergent relationship in which the employees' roles emerge out of the work itself. Rather than specific job requirements and specific tasks to be performed, employees creatively interact with each other and with the environment and out of this interaction their roles evolve. In these interactions, the employees use their talents and skills to develop their roles in response to the changing environment in which they work and, in the process, they help the organization to adapt to its environment. The organization enables the employees to evolve their work by creating an environment within which employees are free to explore and try new ways of performing their activities. This freedom is structured and coordinated throughout the organization in the clear understanding of the mission and vision and values of the organization and organizational rules that structure the work and innovation. Employees are kept informed about the status of the organization and, using this information as the basis for their activities, the employees creatively engage with patients and customers and other employees to manage the work and to respond to changes that occur. Each day as the people within the system respond to events and make decisions, the organization emerges organically from their activities. This emergent metaphor of work and workers provides a new and challenging view of healthcare organizations that offers an alternative to the 20th century mechanistic view.

The metaphor of control describes the essential nature of 20th century healthcare leadership as represented in the leadership transition. White-coated professionals with powerful pens dictated the care of patients to white-uniformed nurses who directed activities of the compliant patients and the supporting workers. At the top of the operational bureaucracy, hospital administrators directed the activities of department managers, who controlled the work of their employees. The control metaphor describes leaders as the creators of the structures of organizations and the managers of the work because they possess the knowledge to make it function efficiently. They see what needs to be done and they have the information to know what needs to change to maintain the organization.

Though the traditional image of control is a powerful metaphor, a new 21st century generative metaphor of trust challenges this older image. The expansion of structures of healthcare organizations to accommodate systems of care and the emergence of new disciplines delivering care in new ways require a new leadership metaphor of trust. Leadership as trust rather than control recognizes the fundamental inability of medical or administrative leaders to see enough and to know enough to control their organizations. Complex adaptive systems force leadership to trust in the nature of these systems to evolve and grow and develop in response to their environments and in the ability of employees to actively participate in creation and management of this evolution. Leadership expresses trust through open communication about all aspects of the organization and support for the work of employees in their efforts to live the values and to fulfill the mission that structures their activities. Trust as a metaphor for leadership moves the organization to a new understanding of this important role in the 21st century and supports the exercise of leadership beyond individuals with power. The metaphor of trust characterizes the transition of the nature of leadership from a position of power in an organizational chart to the reality of leadership that emerges whenever someone sees a need within the organization and takes the initiative to respond to the need.

The metaphor of centralized innovation in the innovation transition corresponds to the bureaucracy of the 20th century healthcare organization and to the understanding of leadership inherent in that model. Because only the senior leaders had the access to organizational information and knowledge about the community, they designed and directed new changes that the workers were to implement. They viewed innovation as their responsibility and their role. As ideas and new ways of working developed in the central leadership, they used the bureaucracy to push the innovation out to workers through the well-defined hierarchy and departmental structure of the organization.

The centralized innovation metaphor no longer serves as a useful image in the light of 21st century healthcare organizations that must respond to internal and environmental changes that are far too complex and occur far too quickly to depend on a central group. Adaptive innovation serves as a powerful generative metaphor for the 21st century to challenge the inadequate image of centralized innovation. This new metaphor focuses on innovation as a natural adaptive response of the organization to changes encountered in the process of work and in the environment. This adaptive response originates spontaneously at the point where the work is performed and the need for innovation can be recognized. Shifting from the bureaucratic centralized innovation to a metaphor of adaptive innovation encourages and supports the creation of new ideas by everyone in the organization, particularly at the point of interface with customers and the environment. This metaphor strongly challenges the older model and communicates a new understanding about innovation. It should occur wherever there is an impetus for change as part of the work for everyone in the 21st century healthcare organization. This metaphor serves as a tool for leadership to encourage employees to become innovative and refutes the previous image that innovation is only the responsibility of senior leadership. It is an image that promotes innovation as real-time adaptation to meet the needs of patients and customers.

In the production method transition, the metaphor of the 20th century craftsman image of the physician providing care to his patient continues to resonate strongly within healthcare organizations and patients. This image fits with the ideals of individualism, personal initiative and industry that are part of the overall 20th century American experience. Many aspects of healthcare organizations not only support this metaphor but raise it to the highest levels of any industry. This is evident in the deference paid to the physician by all members of the hospital staff. The almost unquestioning response to handwritten physician orders as directives for managing the care of patients and to physician notes as the interpretation of the patient's condition and response to care strengthen the craftsman image.

For the 21st century healthcare organization, however, the metaphor of the craftsman physician no longer offers a meaningful interpretation of the way that work is performed and that relationships function. A multidisciplinary team is the 21st century healthcare generative metaphor for the production method transition. This new image challenges organizations to recognize that the craftsman physician no longer offers an adequate model for designing work and for building productive relationships. The new multidisciplinary team metaphor inspires all healthcare professions to see themselves as responsible for the work for and the care of the patient. The physician remains the strongest member of the team in terms of legal responsibility and operational influence, but this strength is now part of the strength of the team rather than in opposition to the team. The skills and the knowledge of the physician expressed within the context of a team of professionals serve to provide a structure for the design and delivery of care. The generative metaphor of a healthcare team provides an image of the future that challenges the individual image and helps to build a strong vision of strength in numbers and shared responsibility. American healthcare is struggling to let go of the heroic surgeon and tireless general practitioner, but the future emerges only when 21st century healthcare organizations value each team member and combine their strengths and wisdom with those of the physician to serve the patient.

As powerful as the image of the craftsman physician, the hospital metaphor of the delivery system transition serves to recognize that there was no real sense of a delivery system of healthcare in the 20th century. The hospital stood and continues to stand in many communities as the defining 20th century image of healthcare. As a healthcare factory using scientific medicine to cure illness and heal injuries and improve the quality of life in the community, the hospital as the metaphor speaks to the single recognized source of healing in the same way that a factory in the 19th and 20th centuries was viewed as the source of goods and prosperity. The hospital stood alone in the mind of the community. The hospital as the metaphor for the 20th century healthcare delivery system of the period serves to emphasize this singularity and lack of any type of system of healthcare. For most of the century, it was where science and society found the clearest expression of the hopes and reality of healthcare.

To assist healthcare organizations in developing to meet the demands of the 21st century, the delivery system transition requires a metaphor that speaks to the rapidly expanding diversity of sources and methods for delivering healthcare. The metaphor of the continuum of care serves to challenge the concept of a single source for healthcare and speaks to the nature of healthcare as designed for patients and customers rather than understood from the design of individual organizations. People experience health on a continuum shaped by many factors and healthcare delivery in the 21st century needs to correspond to that continuum image in the understanding of its design and function. The generative image of healthcare as a continuum of care or series of steps that match the stages of health and care that are experienced by patients represents a powerful image of the delivery system as it moves out of the hospital and into multiple locations in the community and the world without a central structure. The value of the generative metaphor of a continuum of care is the sense that healthcare functions within the context of the patient's life and health rather than in an architectural image.

The information system transition metaphor of isolation for the 20th century image of information systems resonates powerfully with anyone who has been part of the evolution of information systems in American healthcare. As profound as the image of a computer is as a metaphor for innovation and information sharing in most of the world, healthcare's experience has been an ongoing clash between the craftsman production method and isolated delivery system and the desire to use information systems to bring it all together. Using isolation as the image for 20th century information systems captures the way it was designed, structured and experienced. Each computer program existed in isolation and was designed to meet the needs of individual departments and functions within healthcare. Since each department stood alone in its unique functions and needs, the computer programs for each department stood alone. There was no need for communication between computers because the computers were only designed to provide specific answers to specific questions or to store specialized information that could be accessed and used or printed to meet the needs of a limited group or department. The limitation of the isolation of healthcare computer programs emerged as the capability of connecting individual computers developed. As the move to the 21st century advances, the image of the isolated computer to generate a specific piece of information has morphed into a computer that can access seemingly unlimited sources of information all over the world. The 20th century image of the lone, isolated computer monitor as a fragment can be seen in the light of the 21st century image of the computer as a connection to the world. The shift from an image of isolation to an image of endless networks is an important generative metaphor because it shapes the way individuals expect information to come to them and to be shared by them with others. It creates dissatisfaction with isolation and lack of information and promotes the sharing and dissemination of information that actually creates the healthcare organization of the future.

Throughout much of history and much of the 20th century, the metaphor for payment for healthcare as presented in the financial transition could be described as fee-for-service. Individuals purchased healthcare services either in barter or with money. The historic image of the farmer paying the physician with a chicken or eggs for the care of his wife during the delivery of a child is part of healthcare's colorful history. In these situations, it was the physician's time and skill that were purchased as there was little else the physician could offer. The specific services paid for by the patient increased with the advent of hospital care, but payment remained fee-for-service. As commercial and governmental insurance dominated in the middle and latter parts of the 20th century, they paid the fees for each service, and individual patients were much less involved. The fee-for-service metaphor for payment provided a useful understanding of the connection between the payment and each of the services provided by the hospital or physician.

In the 21st century, the metaphor that is emerging incorporates the new delivery system of healthcare as a continuum of care and the new financial reality of the patient as a consumer of and purchaser of health services. Within this new environment, the image of consumer health financing provides a strong contrast to the 20th century fee-for-service model. In consumer health financing, the focus is on the consumer of health services more than on insurers and employers. These entities continue to play a significant part, but the consumer is now the one making decisions and selecting what to buy. Rather than individual services, the customers and patients are purchasing health. They are looking for services that protect and promote health as well as healing and curing. They expect to have access to a wide variety of services. Consumer health financing places the emphasis on the consumer as the purchaser and the customer of health services as well as the patient when acute care is required. This new metaphor provides a useful image to guide healthcare organizations in developing the services to meet the needs of new consumers and the financing plans and transparency to make access as easy and seamless as possible.

In the 20th century, the full-length white coat provided an easily recognizable symbol of the unique position of the physician. As noted in the professional transition, the metaphor of autonomy found full expression in the 20th century in the orders of the physician for the care of the patient. Regardless of the cost to the hospital or the difficulty to the staff, the orders of each individual physician were the rules that governed the care of each individual patient. The physician and the physician alone had the ultimate legal right to order treatments and services for patients because the physician was viewed as the only one who had the training and knew the patient's condition. Since other staff had much less training and knew far less about the patient's illness, it was expected that the physician's orders would be carried out. Other services participated in the care of the patient as ordered by and under the direction of the physician. The autonomy of the physician was seldom questioned.

The 21st century requires a new metaphor for the role of the physician within the relational context of the healthcare system, because the complexity of the delivery process, the speed of change and the availability of information would overwhelm the individual physician trying to direct all aspects of care. The generative metaphor of integration rather than autonomy corresponds more closely to a system in which multiple disciplines, including physicians and patients, must work together to care for patients and to respond to the needs of customers. Physicians are now integrated into teams at all levels of the continuum of care. They continue to function as leaders in these teams but the other professionals on the teams with different training and skills than the physicians play a much larger role than in the past and expect to have their perspectives represented in the care of patients. At the same time, integration as a generative metaphor invites the patient and consumers into the discussions between the professionals. Whether as an acute-care patient in the hospital or as a consumer of preventive health training, the individual receiving the care or the services expects to have a strong voice in the design of the plan of care and the delivery of services.

In the metaphor transition, the 20th century has strong metaphors of scientific management and hierarchical bureaucracy that support the metametaphor of the machinery of healthcare organizations. The hospital is the quintessential expression of the solid, mythical modern factory of healthcare that heals injuries, cures disease and protects patients from death. The metaphor of the machine is not so much consciously and overtly referred to in healthcare, but it is the dominant metaphor in the structuring of the operations of healthcare into departments and the transactional relationships of the leadership with staff. Newtonian physics continues to shape organizations in the collective mind of healthcare as it has throughout the 20th century.

In challenging this traditional, albeit subtle, view of the organization as a machine, the 21st century generative metaphor is a much less familiar but much more useful metaphor of the complex adaptive system. As healthcare organizations move through industrialization and begin to travel the paths of the transitions, the complex adaptive system metaphor offers a guiding and motivating image that is far more useful in creating the future than the machine of the past. In this new metaphor, the complexity of health services as denoted by networks and the information flow within a diverse universe of service agencies and professionals is part of the recognized and accepted image of the future that is emerging. This complexity is not viewed as an external threat to the future that must be managed or eliminated, as it is when the machine metaphor is the filter, but rather as an inherent part of it that offers significant opportunities to organizations. The adaptive nature of healthcare captured in the metaphor challenges the bureaucracy of the past and places the focus on the patient and the consumer and the ability of organizations to adapt to their needs and expectations. The adaptive metaphor inspires the creativity of everyone in the organization to see the needs of patients and consumers as opportunities for improving and expanding services at all levels. Finally, the system is no longer a system only on paper in which power is described in boxes and lines that express control of workers expected only to perform tasks and not to innovate or lead. It is a system structured by the mutual acceptance of all its participants around the mission and the vision and the values of the organization. Wherever employees are working or interacting with each other and with customers and patients, the consistent application of mission and the values and the simple rules that operationalize them are the guides that employees use in creating the system. Through these common beliefs and simple rules, the system emerges as the employees create it each day.

5.3 The 21st Century Circle of Care

Industrialized quality and the expansion of information systems in healthcare organizations create the environment for the emergence of a form of healthcare significantly different from what existed in the 20th century. This new form is not so much planned as it is a confluence of factors shaped as much by the behavior of the patient-customers as it is by the agencies that deliver the care. The hospital epitomized 20th century healthcare. In the 21st century, it is a "circle of care" that describes the spectrum of healthcare processes and experiences of patient-customers.

The circle of care comes together as patient-customers challenge healthcare organizations to respond to their needs in a new environment in which cost and access are important values. Beginning with lower costs and easier access, there is a circular movement in the way patient-customers experience healthcare from preventative services with minimal costs to higher acuity care with more intensive services and greater cost and a return to easy access lower cost care with easy access. The circle connects all elements of healthcare together for the patient-customers through a coordinating patient medical portal that provides information and guidance in all the ways to access the systems and the services available. This provides the interactive and direct link between the patient and the system. At the same time, there is a much broader information system within the healthcare organization that creates a seamless tracking process that follows the patient-customer through all the potential contact points and manages the flow of clinical, demographic and financial information to all participating service providers.

In evaluating the needs and expectations of patients, healthcare organizations recognize that costs in the future will be a significant factor for patient-customers. As new insurance plans sponsored by employers require the insured employees to pay high upfront costs, they create empowered patient-customers that will be searching for low cost and high quality. The challenge for healthcare providers is to establish the delivery system that moves with the patient-customers' needs. This will require restructuring of the way services are delivered to reduce costs and improve access and a reconsideration of many routine tests and procedures that healthcare built into an insurance-based system to determine what customers are actually willing to pay for maintaining their health on a routine basis.

For example, in the past, the initial office visit was the point at which people entered into a relationship with a practitioner. In the future, many patients may expect that their medical records from previous providers will be obtained by the new healthcare provider. New patients will expect the information in those records to be used to evaluate current and future needs with few additional tests needed. Many new patients may find the traditional requests by physician offices for annual routine testing and office visits a costly tradition that offers little benefit.

In addition to the restructuring of the traditional services provided in physician offices and hospitals, patient-customers will expect new ways of obtaining services to be offered that make it much easier and less costly to receive healthcare. This will require the new circle of care to bring in Internet technology to provide low-cost online visits and information and walk-in clinics to complement the more traditional services. For patients with minor illnesses, a quick session via a computer or a short walk-in visit to obtain a prescription fits the modern lifestyle much better than struggling to get an appointment with a physician and waiting an extended period of time to actually see a physician.

In the past, many patients sought to maintain relationships with specific physicians or providers to manage their healthcare throughout their lives. In the modern environment the reality is that specialization and the demand for healthcare services make it costly and impractical for most people to maintain access with an individual provider for all aspects of healthcare. Nurse practitioners are providing care in offices. Hospitalists are providing care in hospitals. Physician assistants provide much of the care for surgery patients following surgery. Specialists are engaged for almost all areas of healthcare.

In this new environment, patient-customers are turning to the same processes that industry has used to build brand loyalty. Rather than searching for a specific provider, patient-customers use their purchasing power to encourage healthcare agencies to ensure that all their providers are courteous and competent and responsive to patient needs. With much more of the payment coming from the patient-customers, the demand for excellent service from practitioners carries significantly more weight than in the past when insurers paid for the service.

Beyond the actual services that patient-customers expect and their satisfaction with the way those services are delivered, the availability of information about their financial options will be significantly more important for a much larger group of patient-customers who are managing their insurance through the open market rather than through employers. Healthcare providers will be challenged by patient-customers in the 21st century to pull back the curtain on consumer health financing and to provide the information that makes them effective patient-customers. Providers will need to provide transparency in pricing information and clear descriptions of the services so that patient-customers in the 21st century can make informed decisions on where to receive care and what type of care meets their needs and their ability to pay. All of this information will need to be readily available online to replicate the industry standards of other major online products and services.

Finally, patient-customers looking for healthcare providers that meet their needs will seek out information and resources beyond their communities and, indeed, around the world. Hospitals and other providers have often looked to their primary and secondary markets within their locality for their patient-customers and have sought to shape their services to compete with other providers in the region. Healthcare will be a global market in the 21st century as patient-customers take control of their health and pay directly for the services they receive. They expect local healthcare to compare favorably with highly rated providers around the world. The implications of this development are significant for providers within the circle of care.

For healthcare organizations to succeed in this new environment of patient-customers, global competition and the circle of care, products and services and quality must meet industrial standards. The only way to meet this standard is to fully implement the industrial quality of Lean and Six Sigma and to initiate the transition to the 21st century. The implementation of Lean and Six Sigma, however, forces significant changes in healthcare organizations that occur not as arbitrary steps in a centralized plan but rather as a natural result of the industrialization process.

To apply industrial quality and to improve their processes and services to meet the standards of the circle of care, healthcare organizations begin by identifying their customers, their products, the value that they deliver and the flow of their processes based on Lean and Six Sigma. It is in identifying these key elements of industrial quality that they realize that the traditions and practices of the past are very different from what is needed in the future. Lean and Six Sigma require changes that transform the organizations, because they require the organizations to redefine the fundamentals of the healthcare model. In trying to identify the customer, they realize that the industrial concept of customers never existed in healthcare. The patient looks more like the product and the physician looks more like the customer, but neither actually purchases the product. A new patient-customer definition is needed in this marketplace of healthcare.

These new definitions enable healthcare organizations to effectively use the Lean and Six Sigma structure of define–measure–analyze–improve–control (DMAIC). By applying this improvement methodology and industry standards in all areas of their operations, healthcare organizations transform existing processes to respond to the needs of their newly identified patient-customers.

It is in the pursuit of these improvements that the leaders and quality professionals recognize an inherent resistance in their operations to the types of improvements required by Lean and Six Sigma. The more that they push to improve, the clearer the resistance becomes. The resistance arises in the ten transitions in the organizational, process and cultural areas in the organizations that reflect the traditions and practices and values of the 20th century. These ten transitions become clear as Lean and Six Sigma are applied because they contrast with values and concepts of the industrial quality and resist the improvement efforts. These areas of resistance did not appear until the organizations tried to implement industrialization and then they became evident. Though the effort to understand the new concepts of customers and flow can be difficult for healthcare organizations, the struggle to move forward in the ten transitions is where the real work occurs.

As organizations use Lean and Six Sigma to improve their processes and to progress toward full industrialization, they increase the pressure on the ten transitions to move as well. In the organizational transitions, the need for a transition from the hierarchical leadership structure to a decentralized complex system image occurs when the centralized structure that worked well in the past to manage resources and communication now seems to make it difficult for employees to get work done or to make improvements quickly. The new complexity of the organizations makes it difficult for senior leaders to keep up with new developments. New processes are needed to streamline the flow of resources and to empower employees to make reasonable decisions based on simple rules that reflect the mission and vision and values.

The need to transition from a transactional employee relationship to an emergent relationship comes in the conflict between leadership promoting Lean and Six Sigma improvements versus employees viewing their work as specific tasks that do not involve improvement or changes. To respond quickly and effectively to patient-customers in 21st century healthcare organizations, leadership and employees need a new understanding of their relationship. Leaders need employees to focus on the dynamic needs of patient-customers in whatever work they perform and employees need the freedom to develop their roles as they perform the work in order to be more effective.

The transition from control to trust comes as members of central leadership realize that they are an impediment to the effort to respond rapidly to patient-customers, because of their traditional ways of controlling work and approving changes. Waiting for meetings and approvals slows improvements as the senior leaders delay the responses to gather more information. Recognizing that they cannot control complex organizations, leadership pushes many decisions out to the points where work is performed and encourages employees to work together by supporting their decisions. Authorizing employees to make reasonable decisions based on clear guidelines and communicating support from leadership helps to build a culture of trust and facilitates meaningful changes.

Organizations striving to achieve higher standards of performance and quality, transition from centralized innovation by senior leaders to adaptive innovation by employees. When Lean and Six Sigma improvement efforts focus on patient-customer expectations, employee efforts to adapt to these demands spontaneously generate innovation. As industrialization progresses and employees recognize signals from their patient-customers and support from leadership, the organization moves toward adaptive innovation.

The process transitions, such as the transition from the craftsman to the multidisciplinary team, appear as patient-customer needs, and the complexity of care requires multiple disciplines working with patients and each other to develop care plans and to monitor patient progress. As the focus shifts from the individual physician's preferences and utility as the sole craftsman to the needs of the patient-customers, the organization transitions to team production processes that bring together multiple disciplines and professionals with shared responsibility and accountability.

As patient-customers seek less costly alternatives within the circle of care, the delivery system for healthcare transitions away from the hospital is the focal point for a continuum of care in which multiple other agencies and service providers deliver care at less cost and with high quality. Maintaining the industrial focus on the patient-customers opens the way to a broader understanding of the delivery of healthcare. Lean and Six Sigma improvements use the links between suppliers and customers within the continuum of care to improve efficiency and reduce costs.

Lean and Six Sigma implementation promote improvement throughout the organization and this drives the transition from isolated computers designed for specific tasks to networks with links throughout the organization to make data available as needed. The networks need to provide real-time information about patient-customers and system activities and also provide communication between individuals and groups to support rapid responses and process improvements within the hospital and affiliated organizations. As this transition progresses, it supports many of the other transitions and the overall improvement effort by providing data for decision support.

Improving services to patient-customers through DMAIC in the financial and business aspects of the organizations brings to light the need to transition from simple fee-for-service programs with insurers to consumer health financing that provides the full package of services and information that patient-customers need. The demands for transparency to help these patient-customers manage costs and arrange for payments becomes a significant process improvement effort for healthcare organizations as they move to a new level of partnership with the people who use their services. Innovative packaging of services and creation of all-inclusive pricing with quality guarantees offers consumer health financing that empowers patient-customers to be able to make reasonable decisions in the circle of care.

As industrialization progresses, the cultural transitions appear as leaders and physicians and employees seek to make sense of what is happening in their organizations and in the circle of care. The professional transition from physician autonomy to integration arises from the work of the multi-disciplinary teams and the need to focus on the goals of the patient-customer. Anything that inhibits using the full capabilities of every member of the team to care for the patient-customers becomes an obstacle that must be removed. The industrial focus on the goals of the patient-customers shifts the organization from a culture that supports autonomy and professional deference to a culture that encourages anyone to participate who can assist the patient and the team. Working with physicians to eliminate the symbols of status and professional autonomy promotes the benefits of open expression within the team structure. Shifting the cultural focus away from professional status and autonomy and to integration brings all the disciplines to the table to care for the patient-customers.

Finally, as all the transitions move toward the images of the 21st century, organizations find the transition from the image of scientific machines to complex adaptive systems useful as an overall representation of the transitions. The shift in the overall organization metaphor coincides with the development of the circle of care and the need for a more useful image to reflect the complexity of healthcare, its new adaptive capabilities and its system nature based on shared beliefs and values. In the movement in the organizational and process transitions, the underlying image of the complex adaptive system slowly emerges as organizations move closer to the 21st century end of the transition continuums.

The 21st century circle of care and the implementation of Lean and Six Sigma that support industrialization and the movement in the transitions focus on the new patient-customer as a fundamental part of healthcare and on the role of the healthcare organization, no matter how large, to facilitate the ability of people to help each other. This is at the root of all that we have discussed. When people are ill, the simplest expression of healthcare is to offer whatever is available to ease their suffering and help them to regain their ability to function and to pursue the goals they consider important in their lives.

What makes it so hard to see this simple equation of two people helping each other is the complexity of the organization and machinery that grew up around the healing process throughout the 20th century. When the fundamentals of community healthcare were lost in the science and the technology of the hospital, the machinery came to be the image that we believed reflected the true nature of healthcare. If operating rooms and MRIs and decades of training are required for one person to help another, then it is very difficult not to see the machine as the heart of healthcare.

The ultimate reality of the machine view of healthcare actually appeared in the costs required to support it. If it takes all of the resources of society as a whole to provide healing, then it is possible that we have defined the nature of healthcare in a way that exceeds the means of humanity to support it. It was when we reached this point that the original vision of the relationships that form the foundation of healthcare reappeared in an amazing way. Surprisingly, the healing relationships emerged out of the complexity of the machine. As industrialization pushed the machine image to its full expression and the transitions opened the broken processes of the 20th century, the patient-customers emerged as the true recipients of healthcare services and healthcare organizations recognized their relationship to their patient-customers. Out of the complexity of the full industrialization of healthcare, human relationships and human thoughts emerge from hundreds of thousands of interactions between people delivering and receiving care to form the structure and the values of the 21st century circle of care.

Chapter 6

What Does It All Mean to You?

The 20th century history of American healthcare established the foundation for traditions, practices and values of healthcare. The current industrialization of healthcare using Lean and Six Sigma methodologies initiates a change process within healthcare that leads to a future vision of 21st century American healthcare. Helping you to know the origins and nature of the changes that are occurring and to have a sense of where it is going is what this guide is all about. Healthcare leaders and quality professionals, in particular, need to understand these historic changes.

The best question to ask yourself at the end of this book is, "What does it all mean to me?" What it means depends on your relation to American healthcare. If you are a leader, this guide offers a framework for understanding the current status of healthcare and what you need to do to move into the future. For quality professionals there is a message designed to inspire you to a new determination to move forward with renewed vigor into industrialization, not as contrary to the principles of healthcare but rather as the passage to the future. Finally, if you are a healthcare consumer, this is your guide to why your healthcare looks and acts the way it does today and the role that you play as a consumer to make the future of healthcare fit your needs.

As a healthcare leader with an administrative or clinical background, this guide offers you a brief exploration of the evolution of 20th century American healthcare and the emergence of 21st century healthcare from the perspective of the significant factors shaping the changes that have occurred and a clear understanding of the forces at work in shaping the industry today. This high-level view is designed to orient you to the origins of the many conflicting perspectives and ideas in healthcare that often make it difficult to develop consensus on the way forward. Describing the major transformative forces at work in the country during the past 150 years and seeing these forces within the context of American healthcare open the way for you to engage your associates and employees in a more robust discussion about creating a future for your organization. Tracing the changes occurring in your organization to the larger national changes may provide useful insights in your efforts to adapt to this new environment.

As a leader in healthcare today looking out over the broad expanse of the past and the future, your next steps are amazingly clear. The first step is to assess where your organization stands in relation to the industrialization phase that lies between the 20th and 21st century models of healthcare. If you are moving quickly toward full implementation of Lean or Six Sigma or another type of industrialization model that draws your clinical staff into the customer-driven healthcare of the future, then you are on the right track. If you have not started this phase or are only marginally engaged in implementing industrial quality, it is time to embrace this part of the American healthcare journey and to move forward with implementation of industrial quality into your organization.

For the early adopters of industrialization, the task is to continue that process of implementation and to begin your assessment of the ten transitions to identify how far you have traveled between the 20th century model and the 21st century model of healthcare. As you see the changes that industrialization is making and the challenges that it produces, you need to recognize that this phase of the evolution of healthcare creates the dynamic forces that will transform your organization for the future. You also need to assess your organization's current status in relation to the 20th century model and the progress toward the 21st century model as the transitions appear. By documenting the characteristics of your organization in the ten transitions that reflect the 20th century and recognizing and documenting the images of the 21st century as they begin to appear, you and your organization will be able to map your path to the future. You will also have the emerging images of the future to motivate and guide your employees in moving forward.

If you are a quality professional, this book offers you insights into the role of industrial quality in moving healthcare into the future and strong encouragement for you to work within your organization to promote industrialization as the way forward. This means putting aside your concerns that industrialization is not right for your organization and moving boldly to implement industrial quality. Based on what you have read in this guide, the path to the future passes through industrialization and industrial quality is the way to move forward. Through this process, your organization will embrace data-driven quality defined by your customers and move from waste and inefficiency built on personal preferences of the professional staff to a multidisciplinary team structure where the skills and contributions of everyone are valued.

For quality professionals in healthcare, the demands and opportunities of the future have never been greater or brighter. As industrialization progresses in your organization, the many ideas and techniques that have been a part of industrial quality for years will seem more relevant than ever. You will probably be busier than ever, but busier with a clear view of the future. As the industrialization takes hold, you will be focusing on the ten transitions that appear and represent the signposts of the future. By evaluating the progression of your organization within these transitions and the transitions in the aggregate, you will see the changes that are occurring and the emergence of the changes that need to occur to move your organization into the 21st century.

Finally, if you are a healthcare consumer overwhelmed and frustrated by the state of American healthcare and trying to figure out how it is supposed to work, this guide offers you the hidden insights into the healthcare system today and what it will look like in the future. Of all the people involved in healthcare—and in a real sense all of us are involved in healthcare—consumers are the ones that will ultimately create the future of healthcare. By embracing new technology that gives you more control of your own health and by demanding better services to meet your goals at a reasonable price from the healthcare system, your voice will decide what the future of healthcare will look like and how well it will work. This is a time for consumers to really begin to use their purchasing power and their desires for high-quality service to reshape healthcare to better serve individuals and families and communities.

Looking back on the history of American healthcare, the culture and industry of America and the aspirations of its people are blazingly manifested in the nature of the healthcare organizations and systems that developed. It is probably accurate to say that American healthcare is the quintessential depiction of America in all its many facets. From the villages and communities of its early years, the image of the lone physician appears sitting beside the bed of a patient in studied apprehension of the forces of disease and illness. In the hospitals and universities and scientific research, the seemingly miraculous products of genius and labor appeared to redefine the possible in healthcare. Out of the innovation of industry and the economic desperation of overwhelming costs, the industrialization of healthcare reshapes this vital service to focus on defining and meeting the needs of people seeking care by shifting the focus of the industry from the professionals as the customers to the individuals being served. Finally, a confluence of multiple factors reshapes the perfect machine of industrialization into the complex adaptive system that is the new circle of care.

After reading this guide, if you would like more information, *Mapping the Path to 21st Century Healthcare: The Ten Transitions Workbook* offers a deeper dive into the role of industrialization and the ten transitions that can help you.

References

ACOS (American College of Surgeons). 2006. "The 1919 Minimum Standard Document." https://www.facs.org/about%20acs/archives/pasthighlights/minimumhighlight

ARRA (American Recovery and Reinvestment Act). 2009. US Government Printing Office. http://www.gpo.gov/fdsys/pkg/BILLS-111hr1enr/pdf/BILLS-111hr1enr.pdf

Barrett, F. and D. L. Cooperrider. 1990. "Generative metaphor intervention: A New Approach for Working with Systems Divided by Conflict and Caught in Defensive Perception." *Journal of Applied Behavioral Science* 26 (2): 219–239.

Berwick, Donald M., A. Balton Godfrey and Jane Roessner. 1990. *Curing Healthcare: New Strategies for Quality Improvement.* San Francisco: Jossey–Bass Publishers.

Bonner, Newville B. 1995. *Becoming a Physician: Medical Education in Britain, France, Germany, and the United States, 1750–1945.* Baltimore: The Johns Hopkins University Press.

Burns, James M. 1978. *Leadership.* New York: Harper Perennial Political Classics.

Coleman, Kate, Brian T. Austen, Cindy Brach, and Edward H. Wagner. 2009. Evidence on the Chronic Care Model in the New Millenium. *Health Affairs* 28 (1): 75–85.

Crowell, Diana M. 2011. *Complexity Leadership: Nursing Role in Healthcare Delivery.* Philadelphia: F. A. Davis Company.

Dartmouth Health Atlas. 2014. http://www.dartmouthatlas.org/

DHHS (US Department of Health and Human Services, Centers for Medicare and Medicaid Services). 2012. More than 100,000 health care providers paid for using electronic health records. http://www.businesswire.com/news/home/20120619006144/en/ten0000-health-care-providers-paid-electronic-health

Donabedian, Avedis. 1980. *The Definition of Quality and Approaches to Its Assessment.* Ann Arbor, MI: Health Administration Press.

Galbraith, Alison A., Dennis Ross-Degnan, Stephen B. Soumerai, Meredith B. Rosenthal, Charlene Gay and Tracy A. Lieu. 2011. "Nearly Half of Families in High-Deductible Health Plans Whose Members Have Chronic Conditions Face Substantial Financial Burden." *Health Affairs* 30 (2):322–331 doi: 10.1377/hlthaff.2010.0584

Gilbreth, Frank B. 1914. "Scientific Management in the Hospital." Speech delivered at the American Hospital Association, St. Paul, Minnesota. Retrieved 8/24/2012. https://engineering.purdue.edu/IE/GilbrethLibrary/gilbrethproject/mgmthospitals

Goodwin, C. S. 2013. "Healthcare Organizational Metaphors and Implications for Leadership." D.A. diss. Franklin Pierce University. Proquest (3567804). http://gradworks.umi.com/35/67/3567804.html

Harry, Mikel and Richard Schroeder. 2006. *Six Sigma: The Breakthrough Management Strategy Revolutionizing the World's Top Corporations.* NY: Crown Business.

Howell, Joel D. 1995. *Technology in the Hospital: Transforming Patient Care in the Early Twentieth Century.* Baltimore: The Johns Hopkins University Press.

IOM (Institute of Medicine). 1999. *To Err Is Human: Building a Safer Health System.* Washington, DC: The National Academies Press.

———. 2001. *Crossing the Quality Chasm: A New Health System for the 21st Century.* Washington, DC: The National Academies Press.

———. 2012. *Best Care at Lower Cost: The Path to Continuously Learning Health Care in America.* Washington, DC: The National Academies Press.

———. 2013. *Variation in Health Care Spending: Target Decision Making, Not Geography.* Washington, DC: The National Academies Press.

Kenney, Charles C. 2008. *The Best Practice: How the New Quality Movement Is Transforming Medicine.* New York: Public Affairs.

Lakoff, George and Mark Johnson. 1980. *Metaphors We Live By.* Chicago: The University of Chicago Press.

Lindberg, Claire, Sue Nash and Curt Lindberg. 2008. *On the Edge: Nursing in the Age of Complexity.* Bordentown, NJ: Plexus Press.

Lohr, Kathleen N., ed. 1990. *Medicare: A Strategy for Quality Assurance, Volume 1*. Committee to Design a Strategy for Quality Review and Assurance in Medicare, Institute of Medicine. Washington, DC: The National Academies Press.

Morgan, Gareth. 1993. *Imaginization*. Newberry Park, CA: Sage Publication.

———. 2006. *Images of Organizations*. Thousand Oaks, CA: Sage Publications.

Office of Legislative Counsel. 2010. Patient Protection and Affordable Care Act Health-Related Portions of the Health Care and Education Reconciliation Act of 2010. http://housedocs. house.gov/energycommerce/ppacacon.pdf

Ohno, Taiichi. 1988. *Toyota Production System: Beyond Large-Scale Production*. New York: Productivity Press.

Roguin, Ariel. 2006. "Rene Theophile Hyacinthe Laënnec (1781–1826): The Man behind the Stethoscope." *Clinical Medicine & Research* 4 (3): 230–235. www.ncbi.nlm.nih.gov/pmc/articles/PMC1570491/pdf/0040230.pdf

Rosenberg, Charles E. 1987. *The Care of Strangers: The Rise of America's Hospital System*. New York: Basic Books.

Schön, Donald A. 1979. "Generative Metaphor: A Perspective on Problem-Setting in Social Policy." In *Metaphor and Thought*, edited by Andrew Ortony, pp. 254–283. Cambridge, UK: Cambridge University Press.

Sollecito, William and Julie K. Johnson. 2013. *McLaughlin and Kaluzny's Continuous Quality Improvement in Health Care* (4th ed.). Burlington, MA: Jones & Bartlett Learning.

Starr, Paul. 1982. *The Social Transformation of American Medicine*. New York: Basic Books.

———. 2011. *Remedy and Reaction: The Peculiar American Struggle over Health Care Reform*. New Haven, CT: Yale University Press.

Stevens, Rosemary. 1998. *American Medicine and the Public Interest: A History of Specialization*. Los Angeles: University of California Press.

———. 1999. *In Sickness and in Wealth: American Hospitals in the Twentieth Century*. Baltimore: The Johns Hopkins University Press.

Taylor, Frederick W. 1911. *The Principles of Scientific Management*. Public domain books, Kindle edition. Amazon Digital Services.

Thomasson, Melissa. 2003. "Health Insurance in the United States."
EH.Net. (March) http://eh.net/encyclopedia/health-insurance-in-
the-united-states/

Uhl-Bien, Mary and Bill McKelvey. 2008. "Complexity Leadership
Theory: Shifting Leadership from the Industrial Age to the
Knowledge Era." In *Complexity Leadership: Part 1: Conceptual
Foundations*. Edited by Mary Uhl-Bien and Russ Marion,
pp. 185–224. Charlotte, NC: Information Age Publishing.

Wheatley, Margaret. 1992. *Leadership and the New Science: Learning
about Organizations from an Orderly Universe*. San Francisco:
Berrett–Koehler Publishers.

Womack, James P., Daniel T. Jones and Daniel Roos. 2007. *The
Machine That Changed the World: The Story of Lean Production—
Toyota's Secret Weapon in the Global Car Wars That Is Now
Revolutionizing World Industry*. New York: Free Press.

Zimmerman, Brenda. 2011. "How Complexity Science Is Transforming
Healthcare." In *Sage Handbook of Complexity and Management,*
edited by Peter Allen, Steve Maguire and Bill McKelvey.
Thousand Oakes, CA: Sage Publications.

Zimmerman, Brenda, Paul Plsek, and Claire Lindberg. 2001.
*Edgeware: Lessons from Complexity Science for Healthcare
Leaders* (2nd ed.). Bordentown, NJ: Plexus Institute.

Index